Model Essays for IB and A Level Economics

GLOBAL ECONOMY Volume 1

Kelvin Hong

Jubilee Kua

First Printing: 2022

ISBN 978-981-18-5495-8

Edventures Pte Ltd

Singapore

www.TheEconomicsTutor.com

9 789811 854958

PREFACE

This book answers 20 key examination questions across the entire Global Economy syllabus, which encompasses both International Trade and Development, and was created to provide students with the ability to excel in their examinations.

Very often, students are unable to provide step-by-step explanations and relevant evaluation points, which are essential to scoring in examinations.

By studying through the model essays provided in this book, students will be able to better understand the various economic concepts covered in the Global Economy syllabus. The powerful diagrammatic analyses provided will also train students to illustrate economic concepts logically, and enable them to use such diagrams for analyses in a more effective and concise manner.

The questions are mostly adapted from past IB examination papers. However, they are also very applicable to the A Level examinations.

We hope that students will now see great hope in scoring very well for their essay papers.

Kelvin Hong & Jubilee Kua

Table of Contents

1. Explain two composite indicators that are useful in measuring economic development. (10)

Introduction

1. "Economic development" refers to a sustained improvement in the standard of living (SOL) of residents in a country. Both the material and non-material SOL of residents are taken into account.

2. The material SOL of residents refers to the quantity of goods and services available to the population for consumption. It is typically measured via real national income per capita.

3. On the other hand, factors affecting the non-material SOL are more intangible aspects that contribute to quality of life. They are usually measured by health, environment, education and other indicators.

4. Composite indicators, unlike single indicators, use more than one measure to ascertain the level of economic development of a country; a country's performance across an assortment of single indicators is calculated to give a single combined figure.

5. Two such composite indicators are the Human Development Index (HDI) and Happiness Index.

Composite Indicator 1: Human Development Index (HDI)

1. The HDI is a composite indicator that measures economic development across three different dimensions: Purchasing-Power-Parity-adjusted real GNI per capita (material SOL), Life Expectancy at Birth (non-material SOL: health indicator), and Mean and Expected Years of Schooling (non-material SOL: education indicators).

2. A single figure is derived and can then be used for comparison between countries, as well as for a particular country, across a certain time period.

3. In 2019, Norway ranked first with a HDI of 0.957, followed closely by Ireland and Switzerland tied with 0.955. In contrast, the Central African Republic and Niger had the lowest HDI figures, 0.397 and 0.394 respectively.

4. Comparing the breakdown of the data between the Netherlands and Australia who were both ranked 8th with HDIs of 0.944, the Netherlands' PPP-adjusted real GNI per capita at $57,707 (2017 $PPP), was much higher than that of Australia's at $48,085 (2017 $PPP).

5. The differences in PPP-adjusted real GNI per capita suggest that the average income earned by a resident of the Netherlands, regardless of where the income was generated, is much higher than that earned by the average Australian. The PPP-adjustment signifies that differences in the cost of living between the Netherlands and Australia have already been factored into the data.

6. Hence, the average Netherlander likely has a higher level of purchasing power, and can likely purchase a higher quantity of goods and services compared to Australian residents. The average Netherlander likely has a higher material SOL than the average Australian.

7. However, both countries have the same HDI score and ranking, due to Australia surpassing the Netherlands in the non-material SOL indicators: "Life Expectancy at Birth", "Expected Years of Schooling", and "Mean Years of Schooling".

8. The "Life Expectancy at Birth" in the Netherlands is 82.3 while in Australia, it is slightly higher at 83.4. Hence, Australia surpasses the Netherlands' by more than one year's life expectancy, though on the whole, the two figures are not very far apart and are both considered high, suggesting that each country's provision of healthcare services and facilities are not drastically different from each other.

9. On the contrary, although Australia only has a very slight edge when it comes to the "Mean Years of Schooling" (Netherlands: 12.4, Australia: 12.7), the number of "Expected Years of Schooling" between the two countries differ to a larger extent. Netherlands' figure stands at 18.5 years while Australia's stands at 22.0. This suggests that Australian residents may have greater access to education opportunities. As education is seen as a critical enabler to a better life, this explains why overall, Australia is considered on par with the Netherlands despite the much higher average income in the latter.

10. As can be seen, the HDI harbours significant strengths in being able to provide an avenue for accurate and comprehensive cross-country comparison of economic development. It can also be used to track the progress of a single country's change in economic development over a particular period of time.

11. The HDI also shows that a higher real national income per capita, though advantageous, will not necessarily translate into a higher standard of living, due to other non-material factors that need to be considered.

<u>Composite Indicator 2: Happiness Index</u>

1. The Happiness Index is released annually in the World Happiness Report, a publication of the United Nations Sustainable Development Solutions Network.

2. It ranks 156 countries' citizens on their level of national happiness, as well as 117 countries on the level of their immigrant's happiness. The level of happiness is measured by citizens' or immigrants' own perceptions and ratings of life in the country. This section will focus on how the citizens' perceptions and ratings are recorded.

3. With regards to the overall national happiness score, respondents are asked to imagine a ladder with steps numbered 0 to 10, with 0 representing the worst possible life, and 10 representing the best possible life. They are then asked which step of the ladder they feel they are currently at. The overall happiness score is thus an average of the responses to this life evaluation question.

4. In addition, respondents are asked for their perceptions of certain variables that correlate with a certain standard of living. These include: "Social Support", "Freedom to Make Life Choices", "Generosity", and "Perceptions of Corruption".

5. For example, under "Freedom to Make Life Choices", the final figure is calculated via the national average to the question: "Are you satisfied or dissatisfied with your freedom to choose what to do with your life?"

6. Additionally, data for the variables "Real GDP per capita" and "Healthy Life Expectancy" is extracted from statistical tables in other existing reports. For instance, figures for Healthy Life Expectancy at Birth are based on statistics from the World Health Organisation.

7. Data collected from all respondents is then used for cross-country comparison, and for analysing respective countries' own trends over a particular period of time.

8. In 2019, the Happiness Index scores of the top three countries were as follows: Finland (1st) with an overall score of 7.769, Denmark (2nd) with an overall score of 7.600, and Norway (3rd) with an overall score of 7.554.

9. In 2019, the Happiness Index scores of the bottom three countries were as follows: Afghanistan (154th) with an overall score of 3.203, the Central African Republic (155th) with an overall score of 3.083, and South Sudan (156th) with an overall score of 2.853.

10. In contrast to the HDI, the Happiness Index considers a lot more social-relational aspects, taking into account how life is perceived and felt by citizens and immigrants. While deeper insights can be gleaned through the Happiness Index, it must also be noted that survey results and perceptions need not always be accurate and can even be volatile.

11. Furthermore, the national happiness figures of citizens and immigrants can be compared, giving governments an understanding of how they can enact policies to better the lives of the immigrants as well.

2. Using real world examples, explain the Theory of Comparative Advantage. (10)

Introduction

1. Comparative Advantage (CA) refers to the ability of a country to produce a good or product at a lower opportunity cost than another.

Explanation

1. According to the Theory of CA, a country should specialise in the production and exportation of goods that it has CA in, while importing goods which it does not have CA in. This would enable both countries to enjoy a combination of goods and services beyond what is attainable by its own Production Possibility Curve (PPC).

2. Differences in CA arise from differences in factor endowments possessed by firms in different countries. This results in different opportunity costs involved in the production of a particular good.

3. For example, suppose China could split its factor inputs equally to produce only computers and milk products, and could produce a total of 90 computers and 30 units of milk products, China's opportunity cost of producing 1 computer would only be ⅓ units of milk products, while its opportunity cost of producing a unit of milk products would be 3 computers.

4. Likewise, suppose the USA split its factor inputs equally to produce only computers and milk products, and could produce a total of 30 computers and 90 units of milk products at any one time. The USA's opportunity cost of producing 1 computer would be 3 units of milk products, while that of producing 1 unit of milk products would be ⅓ of a computer.

5. This assumes homogeneity and perfect mobility of resources in both countries.

	Computers (units)	Milk Products (units)
China	90	30
USA	30	90
World Output	120	120

Fig 1: Production and Consumption prior to Specialisation and Trade

6. In accordance with the Theory of CA, the USA should specialise in producing milk products, and China should specialise in producing computers. This is

rooted in reality, as the opportunity cost needed to assemble computers in factories is usually lower in China due to cheaper manpower and other factors inputs like the materials and parts required, whereas that of producing milk products is lower in the USA, in part due to the abundance of grazing land which supports the large scale rearing of cows on many farms.

7. Hence, China imports many milk products like skim milk powder and fluid milk from the USA, while the USA imports computers from China. In 2020, the USA imported $92.4 billion in computers, with the majority $48.9 billion worth of computers imported from China alone.

8. Both countries would then produce a greater total combined world output of computers and milk products, compared to without specialisation. China would produce 180 computers, while the USA would produce 180 units of milk products. This would make the new total world output for computers and milk, 180 each, whereas that prior to specialisation was 120 units of each good.

	Computers (units)	**Milk Products (units)**
China	180	0
USA	0	180
World Output	180	180

Fig 2: Production after Specialisation

9. Following specialisation, countries would establish the terms of trade (TOT), or the rate at which one product can be exchanged for another.

10. In order for the TOT to be mutually beneficial, it must lie between the limits imposed by each country's opportunity cost ratios. Countries would then be able to enjoy a combination of goods and services beyond what is attainable by its own PPC.

11. In this example, the USA's opportunity cost ratio is 1 computer : 3 units of milk products. The USA will therefore not export more than 3 units of milk products for every computer imported from China because if that were the case, the USA would be better off producing computers herself.

12. Similarly, China's opportunity cost ratio is 1 computer: ⅓ units of milk. Hence, China would not accept less than ⅓ units of milk products in exchange for a computer, because if that were the case, China would be better off producing milk herself.

13. The terms of trade for a unit of computer would thus be ⅓ units of milk products < 1 computer < 3 units of milk products. Similarly, that for a unit of milk products would be ⅓ computer < 1 unit of milk products < 3 computers.

14. Assuming a TOT of 1:1, suppose China exports 50 units of computers to the USA in exchange for importing 50 units of milk products from the USA. China will now have 130 units of computers and 50 units of milk products, and the USA will have 50 units of computers and 130 units of milk products.

	Computers (units)	**Milk Products (units)**
China	180 - 50 = **130**	0 + 50 = **50**
USA	0 + 50 = **50**	180 - 50 = **130**
World Output	180	180

Fig 3: Consumption after Trade

15. Hence, by specialising in the production and exportation of goods that it has CA in, and importing goods that it does not have CA in, both China and the USA can enjoy a greater combination of goods beyond what is attainable by their own PPC.

3. Using real world examples, explain why countries trade. (10)

Introduction

1. Trade refers to the exchange (sale and purchase) of goods and services internationally.

Reason 1: Greater Consumption of Goods and Services

1. Comparative Advantage (CA) refers to a country's ability to produce a good or product at a lower opportunity cost. According to the Theory of CA, a country should specialise in the production and exportation of goods that it has CA in, while importing goods that it does not have a CA in. In this way, countries would be able to enjoy a combination of goods and services beyond what is attainable by their own Production Possibility Curve (PPC).

2. Differences in CA arise from the differences in factor endowments possessed by different countries. This results in different opportunity costs involved in the production of a particular good.

3. For example, comparing Thailand and Singapore, Thailand has a CA in producing rice due to its favourable climate, labour force and large plots of hilly land. This contrasts with Singapore, who has a CA in producing high value-added products like biomedical goods, due to its skilled workforce, numerous foreign direct investments by multinational corporations (MNCs), and areas dedicated to intensive research and development like Science Park, and the functional grouping or clustering of centres in One-North comprising Biopolis (for Biomedical research), Fusionopolis and Mediapolis.

4. If Singapore split its factor inputs equally to produce only rice and biomedical goods, suppose it could produce a total of 30 units of rice and 90 units of biomedical goods at any one time. Singapore's opportunity cost of producing 1 unit of rice would be 3 units of biomedical goods, while that of producing 1 unit of biomedical goods would be ⅓ units of rice.

5. Likewise, if Thailand could split its factor inputs equally to produce only biomedical goods and rice, suppose it could produce a total of 90 units of rice and 30 units of biomedical goods. Thailand's opportunity cost of producing 1 unit of rice would only be ⅓ units of biomedical goods, while its opportunity cost of producing a unit of biomedical goods would be 3 units of rice.

6. This assumes homogeneity and perfect mobility of resources in both countries.

7. In accordance with the Theory of CA, Singapore should specialise in producing biomedical goods, and Thailand should specialise in producing rice. Both countries would then produce a greater total combined world output of biomedical goods and rice than before, without specialisation.

8. As such, Singapore would produce 180 units of biomedical goods and 0 units of rice, while Thailand would produce 180 units of rice and 0 units of biomedical goods. Prior to specialisation, the total world output for each of biomedical goods and rice was 120 units. Therefore, with specialisation according to CA, the total quantity of goods and services produced by both countries would exceed that initially produced before specialisation.

9. Following specialisation, countries would establish mutually beneficial terms of trade (TOT) - the rate at which one product can be exchanged for another that is in between the opportunity cost of producing the good for both countries. Countries would then be able to enjoy a combination of goods and services beyond what is attainable by their own PPC.

<u>Reason 2: Greater Variety of Goods and Services</u>

1. Besides enjoying a greater quantity of goods, consumers would be able to enjoy greater varieties of the good too. This will increase the number of choices given to consumers to suit their differing tastes and preferences.

2. For instance, instead of only enjoying their own domestically-grown Washington Navel, Valencia and Hamlin oranges, they can now enjoy Europe's Arancia del Gargano, Arancia di Ribera and Arancia Rossa di Sicilla, as well as other countries' varieties of oranges, through trade.

3. In the Market for Cars in Japan, the Japanese consume not just home brands like Honda and Toyota, but also BMW from Germany, Ford from the USA and Hyundai from Korea.

4. Hence, with trade, the variety of goods and services available in the domestic economy increases as well. This would appeal to consumers with different tastes and preferences.

<u>Reason 3: Trade Boosts Economic Growth</u>

1. With widened access to more markets, there is an increase in demand for the exports of the domestic country. This would increase the quantity of exports sold, increasing export revenue and net export revenue (X-M), ceteris paribus.

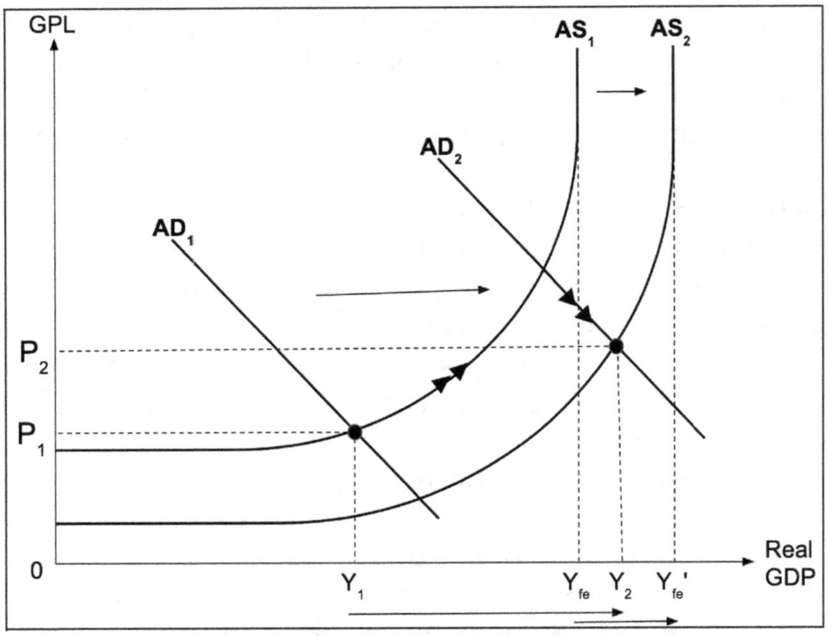

Fig 1: Increased AD from Trade

2. As (X-M) is a component of Aggregate Demand (AD), the increase in (X-M) would cause AD to shift rightward from AD_1. Firms face an unplanned fall in inventory, causing them to hire more factors of production, including workers, to increase production and increase real output. This gives rise to the multiplier effect with one man's spending becoming another's income. Alternate cycles of spending and income generation cause a multiplied increase in AD from AD_1 to AD_2, and a more than proportionate increase in real Gross Domestic Product (GDP) as well.

3. The SRAS and LRAS may also shift downward and rightward respectively. Domestic firms can now import cheaper factors of production from other countries. For example, with trade, the USA imports cheaper steel and construction materials from China, allowing costs of production to decrease. This causes the economy's Short Run Aggregate Supply (SRAS) to increase, shifting downwards and enabling the General Price Level (GPL) to fall in the short run, curbing the effects of cost-push inflation.

4. Simultaneously, since domestic firms are often forced to lower their prices to match the world price for each good to be able to compete on a global scale, they are forced to innovate to improve their production processes and become more efficient. This increased competition for firms could give rise to more sophisticated production techniques, enabling more output to be produced with fewer resources, shifting the LRAS rightward, causing full employment output to increase from Y_{fe} to Y_{fe}'.

5. The combined increase in SRAS and LRAS thus results in an outward shift of the Keynesian AS curve from AS_1 to AS_2.

6. Overall, the real GDP as a result of increases in the AD and AS curves, increases from Y_1 to Y_2.

7. Hence, opening the country to trade also enables greater sustained and non-inflationary economic growth. Actual and potential economic growth can be achieved, while the increased spare capacity and full employment level reduces competition for scarce factors of production, helping ease demand-pull inflationary pressures as the economy grows.

4. Using real world examples, discuss the possible measures a government can implement to correct a Current Account deficit. (15)

Introduction

1. The Current Account (CA) is one of three accounts in the Balance of Payments (BOP), which is a record of all economic transactions taking place between residents of a country and other countries, usually over a year, encompassing all payments received from other countries (inflows or credit) and all payments made to other countries (outflows or debit).

2. The CA is the sum of the Balance of Trade (net export revenue), net income flows (comprising dividends, profits, interest, and rent), and net current transfers (one way monetary transfers like government aid and remittances).

3. As the Balance of Trade (BOT) is usually the largest component of the Current Account, a CA deficit usually occurs when export revenue (X) earned, is smaller than import expenditure (M).

4. Government policies would therefore typically aim to either increase export revenue, decrease import expenditure, or achieve some combination of both.

Policy 1: Depreciation Exchange Rate Policy

1. To increase export revenue and decrease import expenditure, the government can depreciate the exchange rate, which is the price of a country's currency in terms of another foreign currency. During his term, President Trump advocated depreciating the United States Dollar (USD) against other major currencies.

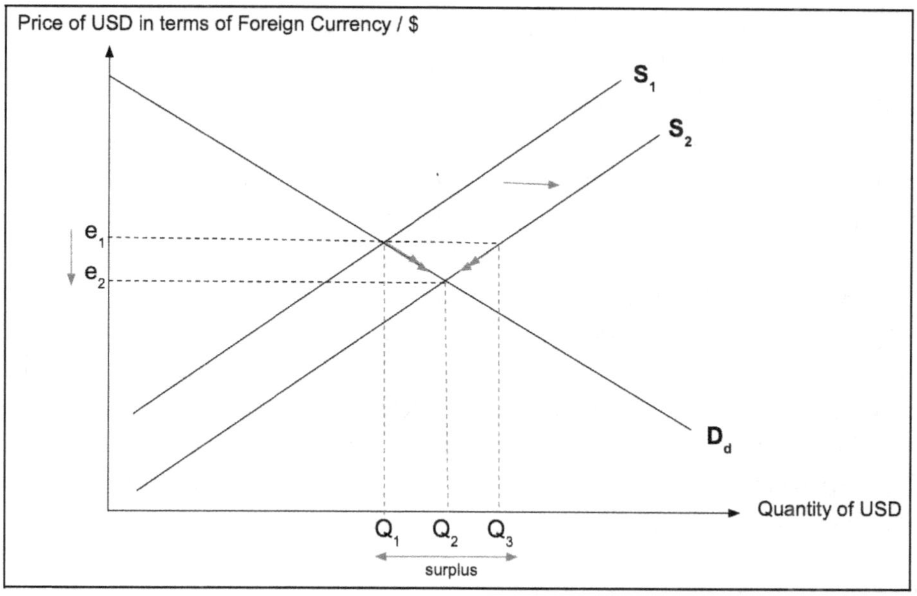

Fig 1: Depreciation Exchange Rate Policy

2. In order to depreciate the USD, the US could sell USD in the FOREX market in exchange for foreign currencies, increasing the supply of USD from S_1 to S_2.

3. Assuming a constant demand for USD, a surplus of Q_1Q_3 for USD would be created at the original exchange rate e_1, putting downward pressure on the price of the USD. Its value would depreciate from e_1 to e_2.

4. When the value of USD falls relative to other currencies, USA exports would be cheaper in terms of foreign currency. Foreigners would be more willing and able to purchase USA exports. As foreigners increase their demand for American goods, the USA's export revenue will increase.

5. Simultaneously, the depreciation would cause imports into the USA to become more expensive in terms of domestic currency. Assuming $PED_m > 1$, quantity demanded would fall more than proportionately, leading to a fall in (M)

6. As long as the Marshall Lerner Condition where $|PED_m + PED_x| > 1$ holds true, with improvements in the BOT and by extension, the CA, the CA deficit can thus be corrected.

Antithesis 1: Disadvantages due to Depreciation Backfiring

1. Countries may come under fire for keeping their exchange rates artificially low, and may be labelled 'currency manipulators'. This is especially because BOT and CA improvements in one country would likely mean a worsening BOT and CA for others.

2. This may lead to retaliatory action from foreign countries, sparking multiple rounds of competitive devaluation if foreign countries likewise depreciate their respective currencies in a tit-for-tat manner. This would affect international relations while resulting in no improvements in the BOT, as relative prices of imports and exports between countries remain constant, and no overall change in export revenue or import expenditure occurs.

3. The weaker currency may also cause foreign investors to lose confidence and fear further devaluations. This may trigger capital flight in the form of portfolio outflows so as to avoid incurring exchange rate losses on their investments. Furthermore, such exchange rate instability may also deter MNCs from investing in the country and this would cause a deterioration in the country's Financial Account; thus one account of the BOP improves at the expense of another.

Policy 2: Supply-Side Policies (SSPs)

1. Increasing the price and non-price competitiveness of domestic goods would cause the foreigners' demand for exports to increase, and the domestic residents' demand for imports to fall. This would increase the export revenue and decrease the import expenditure simultaneously.

2. In 2007, the USA's CA deficit was 6%, an increase from the 2.4% in 1998. During his term, President Obama believed that the key to America's continued economic prosperity was to compete on a global scale through the development of new products, creation of new industries, and via a spike in scientific and technological innovation.

3. Hence, the Obama Administration implemented an industrial policy which involved the establishment of a National Network for Manufacturing Innovation (NNMI). The NNMI was composed of competitively-selected, independently-managed Institutes for Manufacturing Innovation (IMIs), where each IMI had a focus area - for instance, a particular manufacturing process like additive manufacturing or a process enabling the production of new advanced materials like carbon nanotubes, an enabling technology like nanotechnology, or an industry sector producing medical devices.

4. Lawmakers and administrators picked winners among private projects helmed by various IMIs, and rained large amounts of taxpayer money on them (estimated US $1 billion). This resulted in an increase in the level of innovation and research and development (R&D) activity in the country. This translated into technological innovations which were then incorporated into the production of domestic goods and services.

5. This proliferation in research into cutting-edge technology for product development enabled the quality of American exports to increase, and demand for exports increased. The Bureau of Economic Analysis reported that the trade deficit dropped nearly US $10 billion between May and June 2013.

The increased sale of capital goods like construction equipment and machinery aided the most in lessening the deficit. Overall, the USA was selling "more products made in America to the rest of the world than ever before".

6. As the quality of domestically produced goods increased, Americans also imported fewer foreign-made goods, opting to purchase "made in America" products instead. Demand for imports decreased, decreasing import expenditure.

7. In addition, innovation in the form of streamlining production techniques helps to increase productivity. This allows manufacturing to become more efficient, lowering the unit cost of production and allowing cost savings to be transferred to consumers in the form of lower prices. This causes the quantity of domestic goods demanded to increase, decreasing demand for substitute imports; import expenditure falls.

8. This could also result in foreigners increasing their quantity demanded for exports, given that the exports are now relatively cheaper than before. Export revenue would increase as well.

9. Net export revenue increases, ceteris paribus, causing the BOT and thus CA to improve, resolving the deficit.

Antithesis 2: Disadvantages of Supply-Side Policies

1. The ability of the government to engage in SSPs is largely limited by its government budget. Some administrators opposed Obama's policy at the time, citing the federal government's near US $11 trillion dollar deficit. Should the government lack funds and have to seek loans from public financial institutions, this may crowd out private spending, reducing the level of (I) by firms, and (C) by domestic consumers. As (I) and (C) are components of Gross Domestic Product (GDP), actual economic growth may be hampered.

Policy 3: Expenditure Reducing Methods

1. To reduce import expenditure, the government could aim to reduce the overall level of real income in an economy, via imposing a contractionary fiscal or monetary policy. This would involve increasing direct taxes and reducing government expenditure (fiscal policy) or decreasing the money supply and increasing interest rates to raise the cost of borrowing (monetary policy).

2. In the case of a contractionary fiscal policy with the imposition of higher direct tax rates, households would have lower disposable incomes, causing a decrease in purchasing power, reducing the level of (C) in the economy. Coupled with a lowered level of government spending (G), real GDP would fall.

3. A fall in the level of real GDP would likewise result from the use of contractionary monetary policy, which reduces consumer borrowing to spend on big ticket items (C), and borrowing to finance investment projects (I) by firms.

4. Suppose the economy had been producing at output Y_1. The initial decrease in spending would cause a fall in AD, causing AD to shift leftward from AD_1 to AD_2, causing a decrease in real national income from Y_1 to Y_2.

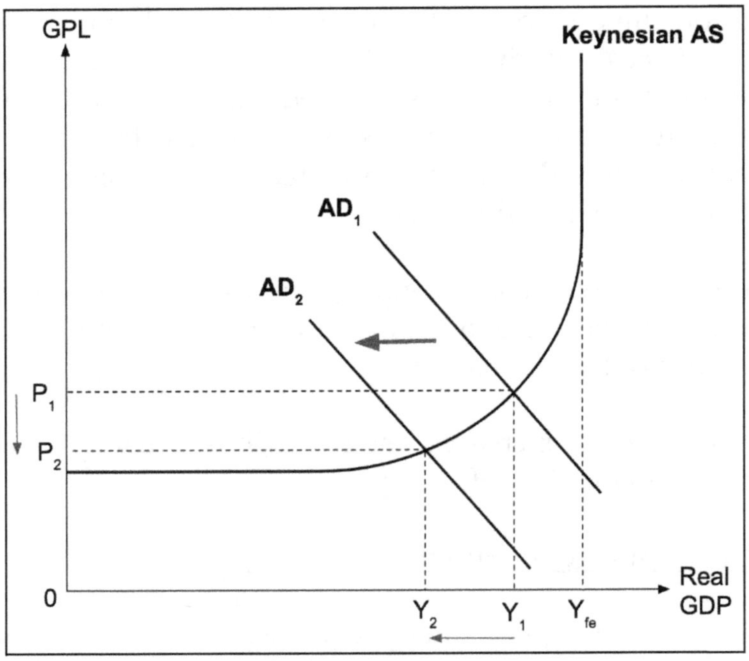

Fig 2: Leftward Shift in AD

5. As real incomes fall, the purchasing power of households decreases, demand for imports would decrease, and fewer imports would be purchased, decreasing (M). A secondary effect may also occur through the fall in the General Price Level (GPL) from P_1 to P_2, as exports would be more competitively priced, increasing the demand for exports by foreigners, increasing (X) as well as reducing the demand for imports, reducing (M). Both effects will improve the BOT and CA.

Antithesis 3: Disadvantages of Expenditure Reducing Methods

1. This policy conflicts with the macroeconomic goal of achieving economic growth, as the real national income decreases as a result of using contractionary fiscal or monetary policies. Unemployment may also increase, thus conflicting with the goal of achieving low unemployment in an economy.

2. This may also lead to deflation or a persistent fall in GPL, accompanied by long periods of recession. For instance, Japan's 'two lost decades' - persistent deflation with low levels of spending and almost zero economic growth.

Concluding Section

1. The government should first aim to understand the root cause of the current account deficit, and then select a policy that would address this root cause. For example, if the problem was a lack of price and non-price competitiveness, SSPs may be a more effective and appropriate policy to ensure that the deficit is resolved in the long term, rather than simply depreciating the exchange rate to provide temporary relief in the short-term.

2. On the other hand, should the issue be an appreciating domestic currency, governments could intervene to depreciate the currency.

3. Finally, the government should weigh the pros and cons of implementing each policy. A multi-pronged approach could be used if appropriate to maximise the effects of the policies. For example, using depreciation/the exchange rate policy as a short-term remedy, whilst implementing SSPs as a long-term policy.

5. Using real world examples, explain possible causes of a trade deficit. (10)

Introduction

1. A country's balance of trade (BOT) refers to its net export revenue, which is calculated by taking the country's total export revenue (X) and subtracting its total import expenditure (M).

2. A trade deficit arises when (X) is smaller than (M).

Possible Cause 1: Appreciating or Stronger Domestic Currency

1. An appreciation of the domestic currency would cause exports to be more expensive in terms of foreign currency, decreasing the demand for these exports and hence decreasing export revenue (X).

2. On the other hand, imports become cheaper in terms of domestic currency, increasing the quantity demanded for imports more than proportionately assuming $PED_m > 1$. This would increase the import expenditure (M).

3. Given the decrease in (X) and increase in (M), the value of (X-M) would decrease, which could result in a trade deficit.

4. For example, the USA has traditionally had a strong and mostly appreciating currency, the United States Dollar (USD). Amidst the continual rise in the value of the USD against other foreign currencies in 2021, the USA "trade deficit in goods mushroomed" as "imports surged and exports slipped", resulting in an even larger trade deficit in 2021.

Possible Cause 2: Greater Real GDP per Capita in Domestic Country

1. If the domestic country has relatively higher levels of real national income per capita compared to foreign countries, its residents would possess higher levels of purchasing power and would be more willing and able to afford imports. This could result in a country's higher demand for imports, relative to foreigners' demand for its exports. Thus, the country's (M) may be higher than (X) earned, resulting in a trade deficit.

2. For example, in 2020, the USA sustained a trade deficit with China; the USA exported only US $125 billion worth of goods to China, while importing US $434 billion worth of goods from China.

3. This could possibly be explained by the fact that in 2021, the USA had a PPP-adjusted real income per capita of about US $60,000 while that of China

was only about US $17,000. The average PPP-adjusted real GDP per capita of the USA was more than three times that of China's. As a result, the USA residents had greater purchasing power and were more able to afford imports than Chinese residents.

<u>Possible Cause 3: Lack of Economic Competitiveness (Price and Non-Price)</u>

1. Countries whose goods lack price and/or non-price competitiveness would see a lower demand for their exports and hence, lower (X) earned.

2. At the same time, there could be high demand by domestic residents for imports with greater price and/or non-price competitiveness compared to the domestic goods, causing a high level of (M). This may lead to a trade deficit.

3. For example, in 2011, Brazilian businesses suffered from rising costs because of high taxes, expensive credit, shortage of skilled labour and infrastructure bottlenecks. This led to the country producing relatively expensive goods amidst a flood of cheap imports. This, among other factors, resulted in Brazil sustaining a US $8.3 billion trade deficit with the USA that year.

[BONUS ANSWER]
<u>Possible Cause 4: Protectionism by Foreign Countries</u>

1. Protectionism involves any attempt by a country to impose restrictions on the open trade in goods and services, and mostly involves imposing trade barriers on imports in order to shield domestic industries from foreign competition. Forms of protectionism include placing tariffs or quotas on imports and subsidising local producers.

2. Should foreign countries impose a tariff for instance, it would make the domestic country's goods less price competitive and there would be a reduction in the demand for exports, reducing (X) earned by the domestic country.

3. The decrease in (X) could result in a trade deficit if the value of (X) becomes lower than that of (M). For example, during his term, President Donald Trump attributed the USA's lengthy trade deficit with China to the latter's alleged unfair protectionism. In 2018, Trump retaliated and imposed tariffs of 25% on Chinese goods.

4. This, among other factors like the slowing global growth, caused China's export revenue to fall; its trade surplus with the USA fell about 10% from 2018 to 2019. Should USA protectionism escalate, China's trade surplus may eventually be wiped out and may become a trade deficit in the future.

6. Discuss the consequences on stakeholders when governments use tariffs to correct trade deficits. (15)

Introduction

1. A tariff is a tax placed on imported goods or services as a form of protectionism, which is any attempt by a country to impose restrictions on the open trade in goods and services, and mostly involves imposing trade barriers on imports in order to shield domestic industries from foreign competition.
2. A tariff can either be levied on a specific or ad valorem basis.
3. A specific tariff refers to a fixed amount of tax per physical unit of the imported good, while an ad valorem tariff refers to a tax that is levied as a percentage of the price of the good.
4. A trade deficit is a situation in which the inflows or export revenue (X) earned is smaller in value than the outflows, or import expenditure (M) spent by the domestic economy. This results in (X-M) having a negative value, causing a trade deficit.

Implementation of Tariff

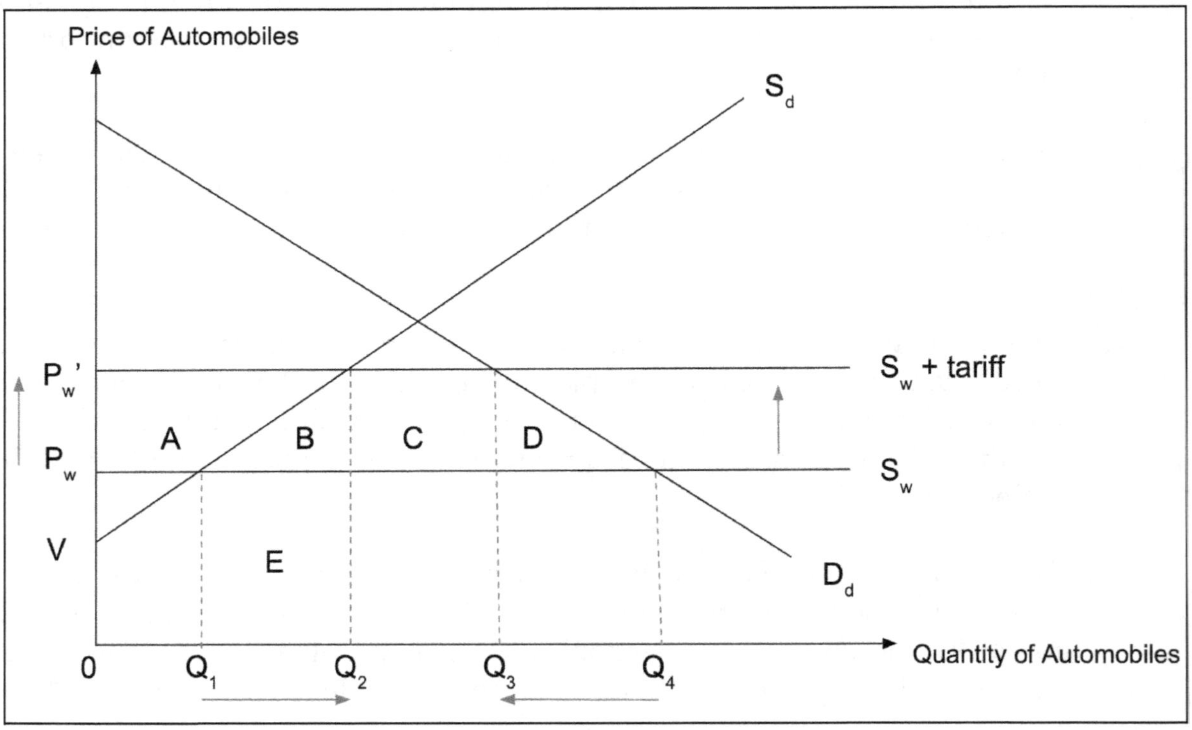

Fig 1: Implementation of Tariff

1. Assuming that foreign firms can supply an infinite quantity of automobiles at the world price P_w, the world supply curve S_w is horizontal, as it is assumed to be perfectly price elastic.

2. At the world price P_w, the automobile quantity demanded is Q_4. The domestic production of automobiles is represented by Q_1, while the excess demand is met by imports of quantity Q_1Q_4.

3. If, in an attempt to correct a trade deficit, the domestic government decides to impose a tariff, the domestic price will rise from P_w to P_w' by the per unit price of the tariff.

4. For example, in 2021, the imposition of a 70,000 peso passenger car tariff in the Philippines to correct the multi-billion trade deficit resulted in increasing prices of automobiles for domestic consumers.

5. At P_w', domestic production rises from Q_1 to Q_2 in accordance with the law of supply, which states that an increase in price of a good would cause an increase in quantity supplied by profit-motivated producers.

6. In contrast, the quantity of automobiles demanded decreases from Q_4 to Q_3 in accordance with the law of demand, which states that an increase in price would result in a decrease in quantity demanded by domestic consumers. The excess demand Q_2Q_3 is then satisfied by imports.

7. The decrease in imports from Q_1Q_4 to Q_2Q_3 would decrease the import expenditure (M). Thus, the trade deficit may be corrected if (M) is reduced to a level lower than (X).

Thesis 1: Positive Consequences on Domestic Producers and Workers

1. The increase in quantity of automobiles supplied by domestic producers from Q_1 to Q_2 suggests a rise in domestic production and output, an increase in the employment of workers (a derived demand), and consequently, a lower unemployment rate.

2. This not only increases the real incomes of domestic households, but also works towards achieving the macroeconomic goal of low unemployment.

3. Revenue earned by domestic firms also increases from $P_w \times Q_1$ to $P_w' \times Q_2$ due to the increase in both price and quantity of automobiles produced. There is also an increase in producer surplus by Area A.

4. Should the automobile industry be an infant industry - a new domestic industry which has not yet had the time to establish itself, it will not enjoy economies of scale and will be unable to compete with foreign firms. Protectionism may thus serve to provide time for the industry to grow so that in future, it is able to compete with foreign firms as it grows in size and innovates. As the infant industry expands, job opportunities are created for workers as well.

<u>Antithesis 1: Negative Consequences on Domestic Producers and Workers</u>

1. If tariffs are levied on many different factors of production, raw materials and intermediate goods - goods used in the production of other goods, this could increase the unit costs of production for various final goods. This could reduce profits for such domestic firms, since profits are the difference between total revenue and total costs.

2. For example, at the height of the USA-China trade war during President Donald Trump's presidency, the USA imposed tariffs on about US $112 billion Chinese imports, including hefty 25% and 10% tariffs on Chinese steel and aluminium respectively.

3. It was reported that the aluminium tariffs also caused around 75,000 job losses in the metal-using industries (industries using metal as a key factor input) in 2019. The trade war as a whole caused the retrenchment of around 175,000 workers by mid-2019 across various industries.

4. Such tariffs also adversely affect the price competitiveness of firms as the increased unit costs of production results in higher prices, hurting export price-competitiveness. Ceteris paribus, these domestic firms' revenue and profits will decrease, adversely affecting the employment of domestic workers as well.

5. Furthermore, imposing tariffs to correct a trade deficit could cause retaliation by other countries in the form of increased protectionism against the domestic country. As the domestic firms' exports likewise become less price competitive or even disallowed from overseas markets, export-oriented domestic firms would earn less revenue and profit as well.

6. All these scenarios could potentially result in shutdown conditions being triggered, forcing some firms to cease operations, and workers to suffer retrenchment.

<u>Thesis 2: Positive Consequences on the Government</u>

1. The government would earn a tariff revenue of Area C. This could be used to finance the provision of more public or merit goods. This, coupled with the protection of the domestic industry against foreign competition, could potentially increase the government's political popularity.

2. The government could also use this tariff revenue to correct its budget deficit and alleviate its own accumulated debt.

Antithesis 2: Negative Consequences on Domestic Consumers

1. Domestic consumers would face increased prices of automobiles at P_w' instead of P_w. Hence, there is a decrease in consumption of automobiles from Q_4 to Q_3, as the increase in price would result in some consumers being unwilling and/or unable to afford automobiles at their new price.

2. There is a loss in consumer surplus of Area A + B + C + D, due to the decrease in quantity consumed by domestic consumers and higher per unit price.

3. This may disproportionately affect lower income households, who usually pay a larger proportion of their income for automobiles as compared to higher income households. With fewer low income households being able to afford automobiles, which may be a necessity in some areas with inadequate public transportation like in some parts of the United States, income inequality widens, as some may even be unable to commute to work to earn a living to pay for basic necessities.

4. If tariffs are levied on many different factor inputs, raw materials and intermediate goods, this could result in an increase in the unit cost of production for various final goods and services. This may lead to cost-push inflation in the economy, adversely affecting consumers who will see their purchasing power eroded further.

Antithesis 3: Negative Consequences on Foreign Producers

1. Foreign producers face a loss in export revenue from the original $P_w(Q_1Q_4)$ to $P_w(Q_2Q_3)$, as the domestic country's import expenditure has fallen. This loss in revenue is due to a decrease in the quantity of automobiles exported, despite the price at which the foreign automobiles are sold at, remaining at P_w. The fall in revenue would lead to lower profits earned.

Antithesis 4: Negative Consequences for Society

1. There is a net welfare loss for society as a whole, consisting of Areas B + D. The welfare loss incurred by Area B is due to the additional higher costs paid by the economy, as the production of quantity Q_1Q_2 shifts from more efficient foreign producers, to less efficient domestic producers. This causes productive inefficiency, as the production cost of Q_1Q_2 units by domestic firms is now equal to Area B + E, but could originally be produced by more efficient overseas firms at the cost of just Area E.

2. The reduction in consumption of quantity Q_3Q_4 due to the increase in domestic price of automobiles, results in the dissipation of consumer surplus of Area D.

3. However, society may also benefit from an increase in the provision of public or merit goods as a result of government revenue earned from the tariff. These benefits, though, are much less certain compared to the welfare loss arising from the tariff, as the former depends on the actual amount that the government chooses to spend on public and merit goods.

Concluding Section

1. In conclusion, the implementation of tariffs brings about many negative consequences for various stakeholders like foreign producers, domestic consumers, and possibly even domestic producers and workers. These harms may actually outweigh the benefits felt by the protected domestic producers and the government.

2. The government should be extremely judicious in choosing which imports to tax, being careful to avoid imposing tariffs on key raw materials and factor inputs, so as to mitigate the detrimental consequences felt by domestic producers and by extension, domestic consumers.

3. Given the many negative consequences, the imposition of tariffs are more justified in the case of correcting dumping activities by other countries as well as temporary short-term measures, for example, to help infant industries.

7. Using real world examples, discuss the consequences of a current account deficit and whether governments should always be concerned. (15)

Introduction

1. The Current Account (CA) is one of three accounts in the Balance of Payments (BOP), which is a record of all economic transactions taking place between residents of a country and other countries, usually over a year, encompassing all payments received from other countries (inflows or credit) and all payments made to other countries (outflows or debit).

2. The CA is the sum of the Balance of Trade (BOT) or net export revenue, net income flows (dividends, profits, interest, and rent), and net current transfers (one way monetary transfers like government aid and remittances).

3. As the BOT is usually the largest component of the CA, a CA deficit usually occurs when export revenue (X) is smaller than import expenditure (M).

Thesis 1: Governments should always be concerned, as a Current Account deficit may suggest a fall in the Balance of Trade, leading to a fall in actual economic growth.

1. Assuming that the CA deficit is due to a trade deficit stemming from a worsening BOT, the (X-M) component of the Aggregate Demand (AD) would be falling. By extension, real Gross Domestic Product (GDP) and actual growth would fall as well.

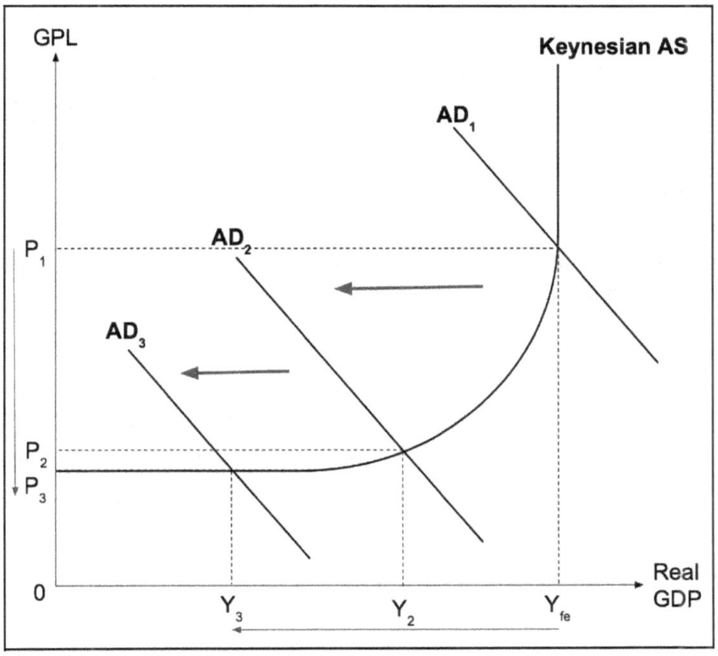

Fig 1: Fall in AD via the Multiplier Effect

2. AD would decrease and shift leftward from AD_1 to AD_2, causing real GDP to fall from Y_{fe} to Y_2, triggering the reverse multiplier effect. As one man's decrease in spending leads to another's loss in income, the initial decrease in (X-M) would result in an unexpected surplus in inventory.

3. As firms decrease their production output of goods and services, fewer workers are hired (derived demand), causing a loss in real incomes. This triggers another round of reduced spending, causing AD to fall further from AD_2 to AD_3, thereby causing production to decrease even further from Y_2 to Y_3, with even fewer workers to be hired and unemployment increasing.

4. Overall, the AD falls more than proportionately to the initial decrease in (X-M) via the reverse multiplier effect, from AD_1 to AD_3, causing real GDP to fall more than proportionately from Y_{fe} to Y_3.

5. Research conducted in 2020 by the Institute of Regional Development at Siauliai University found that in the European Union (EU) countries, a deterioration in the BOT "reduces average economic growth", independent of "whether [the BOT] starts [from a position of] trade deficit or surplus".

<u>Thesis 2: Governments should always be concerned, as a Current Account deficit may lead to a fall in investments in the country, adversely affecting actual and potential growth.</u>

1. As CA deficits can be seen as a sign of weakness in the economy, the 'animal spirits' as stated by Keynes, may plummet as firms may lose confidence amidst the heightened economic uncertainty.

2. Firms, especially multinational corporations (MNCs), will be less incentivised to invest in such countries, or may even pull their long-term investments out of the country, decreasing the level of (I) in the economy. As (I) is a component of AD, actual economic growth will be hindered.

3. For example, Mexico and Thailand experienced CA deficits in 1995 and 1997 respectively. This caused foreign investors to perceive instability, causing investments in the country to be withdrawn.

4. A decrease in (I) could simultaneously lead to decreased capital stock in the economy, including machinery and factories, causing the productive capacity or full employment output of the economy to decrease, and the Long Run Aggregate Supply (LRAS) to also fall. Hence, potential growth is also hindered.

Thesis 3: Governments should always be concerned, as a current account deficit may lead to a BOP deficit and the depletion of FOREX reserves.

1. Given that the BOP consists of the Current, Capital and Financial Accounts, a CA deficit could cause the BOP to worsen, and a BOP deficit to occur. Persistent BOP deficits are typically a cause for concern, due to knock-on detrimental effects on the economy.

2. When a country has a persistent BOP deficit, this means that their payments to other countries (outflows) are greater than their international receipts (inflows). This could deplete the country's Foreign Exchange (FOREX) reserves as they are utilised to finance the BOP deficit.

3. The depletion of FOREX reserves would limit the government's ability to defend the domestic currency against speculative attacks and implement measures like exchange rate policies.

4. This is because a lack of FOREX reserves would hinder the government's ability to sell foreign currencies in order to purchase domestic currency in the FOREX market. Hence, the government will be unable to increase or maintain the domestic currency's value, and the domestic currency will depreciate or devalue.

5. This leaves the economy exposed and vulnerable to speculative attacks. The 1997 Asian Financial Crisis occurred due to Thailand being unable to defend itself against speculative attacks that massively devalued the Thai Baht. As Thailand lacked foreign reserves, it was unable to purchase excess quantities of Baht in the foreign market, causing the currency to devalue. This resulted in the Thai Baht becoming highly unstable, causing foreign firms to put off investment inflows into Thailand, further harming the Thai economy.

6. A lack of foreign reserves may also cause the country to be unable to finance the purchase of imports, which could include basic necessities such as food. This would have severe consequences on the standard of living of its citizens.

Antithesis 1: Governments should not always be concerned, as the Current Account deficit can be self-correcting.

1. As mentioned, the CA deficit may cause a currency depreciation, which could trigger an automatic adjustment process which results in the correction of the trade and CA deficit.

2. This is because as the domestic currency depreciates, exports become cheaper in terms of foreign currency. Foreigners would be more willing and able to purchase exports. As foreigners increase their demand for goods, (X) will increase.

3. The depreciation of the currency would also cause imports to become more expensive in terms of domestic currency. Assuming $PED_m > 1$, quantity demanded would fall more than proportionately, leading to a fall in (M).

4. As long as the Marshall Lerner Condition where $|PED_m + PED_x| > 1$ holds true, the simultaneous increase in (X) and decrease in (M) would enable (X-M) to increase, ceteris paribus, improving the BOT. By extension, the CA deficit can thus be corrected automatically, without government intervention. Hence, governments need not always be concerned about a CA deficit as it is self-correcting.

Antithesis 2: Governments should not always be concerned, depending on the cause of the Current Account deficit.

1. Should the cause of the CA deficit be a lack of price or non-price export competitiveness leading to a fall in demand for the domestic country's exports, the government should perhaps be concerned and enact policies like supply-side policies, to increase the price and non-price competitiveness of such exports. This is because short of working towards increasing the competitiveness of exports, the country will likely face a perpetual CA deficit in the long term.

2. However, if the CA deficit is due to a temporary spike in import expenditure (M), for instance, for countries in the early stages of economic development importing large quantities of capital goods and factors of production, the government may not need to be worried as this will likely resolve with time.

3. For example, between 1965 to 1985, Singapore was starting to industrialise, and the Singapore government had the goal of building a manufacturing base in Singapore. This required many capital goods to be imported. Hence, Singapore incurred CA deficits averaging 10% of GDP, but this did not pose a serious concern to the government, as these were seen as investments to help the economy's productive capacity and future economic growth.

4. Once the factories were up and running, Singapore was able to increase its production output and sell exports, increasing (X) and improving the BOT and CA. Hence, the CA deficit was only temporary and enabled Singapore to achieve long term economic growth, and even a CA surplus down the line.

Antithesis 3: Governments should not always be concerned, as CA deficits may bring about positive consequences under certain circumstances.

1. Assuming that the CA deficit is due to a trade deficit stemming from a worsening BOT, the (X-M) component of the Aggregate Demand would be falling. By extension, real GDP and actual economic growth would fall as well. This may be beneficial in curbing demand-pull inflation and preventing the

economy from overheating, should the economy be operating at or near full employment output.

2. Referring to Fig 1, the economy is originally producing at the full employment output, Y_{fe}. At Y_{fe}, all factors of production are being fully and efficiently utilised at the given level of technology. Any further increases in AD would not translate into an increase in output, but rather cause the General Price Level (GPL) and inflation to rise rapidly. This is because the shortage of factor inputs amidst rising demand by firms would result in firms bidding up the prices of factor inputs to secure them.

3. Hence, in situations like these where the economy is susceptible to overheating and rising inflation, the Current Account deficit works in a manner similar to an expenditure-reducing policy, shifting the AD leftward from Y_{fe} to Y_3 and decreasing the GPL from P_1 to P_3, curbing inflation.

Concluding Section

1. In conclusion, whether the government should be worried about a CA deficit is largely dependent on: the root cause of the deficit, size of the deficit, the nature of the economy, as well as the duration of the deficit.

2. Prolonged, high CA deficits are typically more worrying than temporary, small deficits due to the detrimental knock-on effects on the economy. The former would lead to a prolonged and large depletion of FOREX reserves, a loss of confidence by MNCs, and the subsequent withdrawal of investments which affect both actual and potential economic growth.

3. The root cause of the deficit and nature of the economy in question are also important factors to be considered. For example, should the root cause of the deficit be a lack of export competitiveness, governments should be concerned, especially if the economy is a small, open one, as this may greatly affect the long-term economic growth of export-oriented economies. The government should thus take action to implement measures like supply-side policies to increase the competitiveness of their exports and resolve the CA deficit.. However, this situation may not be as worrying in large, domestic consumption-dependent economies like the USA.

4. Lastly, the consequences of a CA deficit are not always bad, and could be viewed as a beneficial outcome that acts to cool down an overheating economy.

8. To what extent is the key to achieving economic development, reducing income inequality? (15)

<u>Introduction</u>

1. Economic development refers to a sustained improvement in both the material and non-material standard of living (SOL) of a population, which concerns both the economic and social well-being of residents respectively.

2. The material SOL involves the amount of goods and services available for consumption and may be measured by the real national income per capita, while the non-material SOL consists of less tangible, quality of life factors and can be measured by health, environmental, educational, and other indicators.

3. Income inequality refers to the idea that income earned in an economy is not distributed fairly, but rather, concentrated in the hands of a small percentage of top earners in the country, while the lowest income earners earn a much smaller percentage of the total real national income in the economy, and as a result, may be unable to fulfil even their basic human needs.

4. Income inequality is typically measured by the Gini coefficient. The Gini coefficient of a country ranges from 0 to 1, with 0 corresponding to perfect income equality while 1 corresponds to perfect income inequality. The higher the Gini coefficient, the higher the level of income inequality in the country.

<u>Thesis 1: Reducing income inequality is the key to achieving economic development, as the lower income earners are more able to break out of the poverty cycle, achieve greater material and non-material SOL, improving economic development.</u>

1. Reducing income inequality can be achieved via a system of progressive taxation, where the higher-income earners pay a higher proportion of their income in taxes, compared to the lower-income earners who pay a lower proportion of their income or none at all in income taxes. Countries like Singapore, Belgium, Germany, Lithuania, Denmark, Slovenia, and many others use a progressive taxation system.

2. Through the progressive taxation system, the government earns tax revenue that can be redistributed to lower income households. The government could give transfer payments or welfare benefits to lower income households, providing a more targeted means of helping the lower income; alternatively, they could directly provide and/or subsidise merit goods like healthcare and education for the lower income.

3. A transfer payment occurs when the government provides payments to a party (in this case, lower income households), for which no goods or services

are exchanged. In giving the lower income transfer payments and direct subsidies, the government effectively increases their level of real disposable income and purchasing power, ceteris paribus. By being more willing and able to afford goods and services, the lower income households are able to consume more, increasing their material SOL.

4. Additionally, by increasing the lower income's level of real disposable income, they would be more able to break out of the poverty trap.

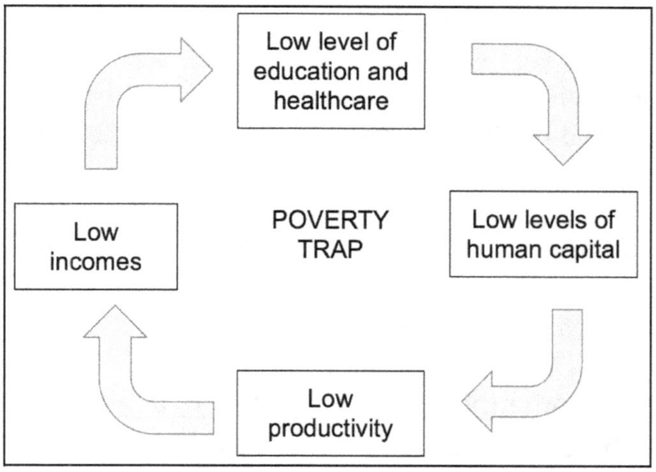

Fig 1: The Poverty Trap

5. As seen in Fig 1, the poverty trap is characterised by a situation whereby low incomes give rise to low levels of education and healthcare due to a lack of affordability. This in turn results in low levels of human capital and hence low productivity, leading again to low incomes. The poverty trap thus depicts a cycle that the poor are unable to get out of.

6. By increasing the lower income earners' levels of real disposable income, households are able to access a greater level of education and healthcare services. With the tax revenue earned from the higher incomers, the government may also choose to directly provide education and healthcare services catered for the lower income households.

7. For example, Singapore's Ministry of Education provides affordable, quality two-year kindergarten services to Singapore Citizens and Permanent Residents aged 5 to 6. This ensures that independent of household income, young children will be able to benefit from a holistic education in their formative years.

8. The government could also establish skills training centres to retrain lower income workers. They would then possess more in-demand, niche skills, greatly improving job prospects, productivity and wages.

9. With regards to healthcare, in the United Kingdom, the National Health Service is a universal healthcare system publicly-funded through taxes.

Healthcare services are available for all, free at the point of need; lower income earners have access to the same level of healthcare as higher income earners within the public healthcare system. This ensures better short and long term health of the lower income, enabling them to lead a healthier life as a whole.

10. Through these policies, the lower income households would be able to break out of the poverty cycle by increasing their levels of education and healthcare, and by extension, enabling them to invest more in human capital, which would lead to greater productivity and higher incomes in the future. This would allow their material SOL to improve.

11. Furthermore, with the lower income households' obtaining greater access to merit goods like healthcare and education, the non-material SOL of the lower income would increase.

12. With the material and non-material SOL of lower income earners increasing, by extension, that of the country would increase as well, enabling economic development to be achieved.

Thesis 2: Reducing income inequality is the key to achieving economic development, as other aspects of the non-material SOL of the lower income earners, and by extension, the country, is improved.

1. Studies from the United Nations illustrate that there is a correlation between income inequality and social stability; a Gini coefficient greater than 0.4 (high income inequality) is a danger to social stability in the country.

2. Thus, by lowering income inequality, there would likely be greater social stability in the country, improving the residents' non-material SOL as public safety is maintained. The opposite of this may be civil unrest when those who are dissatisfied by the lack of inclusive economic growth take to the streets to protest and riot.

3. This issue of income inequality has given rise to political instability in many countries in various regions over the last decade. For example, in 2019 in Chile, a US $0.04 (30 pesos) rise in metro fares caused thousands to take to the streets in protests. Though Chile, with a per capita income of US $15,800 in 2019, was one of 36 members of the Organisation for Economic Cooperation and Development (prosperous nations), it was also the member with the highest level of inequality. About half of Chileans were earning under US $550 a month in 2019, with a 2018 study showing that the richest had an income 13.5 times higher than the poorest. Hence, the rise in metro fare was the breaking point for many lower income Chileans who were already struggling to make ends meet due to high living costs.

Antithesis 1: Reducing income inequality is not the key but rather only one of many factors to consider when striving to achieve economic development.

1. The non-material SOL, and by extension, the level of economic development in a country, is not determined solely by its level of income inequality. Other potential factors that contribute to the level of non-material SOL include (but are not limited to): environmental standards, the level of safety in a country, the presence of civil rights such as the emancipation and empowerment of women, and political stability.

2. Hence, notwithstanding income inequality, there are many other factors which may hinder the road to economic development. In 2022, Azerbaijan was ranked 8th for the countries with the lowest Gini coefficients. However, Azerbaijan has consistently ranked lower in other non-material indicators, like having only 12.9 "Expected Years of Schooling" in 2018, compared to other countries with higher Gini coefficients having close to 20 years. Its 2018 "Life Expectancy at Birth" was 72.9 years, which was lower than many other countries with higher Gini coefficients. This, amongst other factors, caused Azerbaijan to rank only 87th out of 189 countries on the 2018 Human Development Index (HDI), a composite measure of economic development.

3. Furthermore, Azerbaijan is infamous for its issues of domestic violence; as of 2020, around 74.2% of husbands had beaten their wives. There was also a severe shortage of health care centres and women's crisis centres, especially in rural areas. With both petty and violent crime on the streets, local safety in Azerbaijan is in question. Corruption in Azerbaijan was also rampant and occured at all levels in the government, leading to it being ranked 129th worst out of the 180 evaluated countries in the Transparency International's 2020 Corruption Perception Index.

4. Additionally, despite Azerbaijan having the lowest income inequality, in 2020, the country's Purchasing-Power-Parity-adjusted real Gross Domestic Product per capita (PPP-adjusted real GDP per capita) was US $14,431. Compared to the world average PPP-adjusted real GDP per capita of US $18,381, this illustrates that low income inequality does not actually preclude residents in countries like Azerbaijan from being equally poor compared to nations with higher income inequalities.

5. Hence, the key to achieving economic development does not lie in just reducing income inequality per se, but ensuring that the country ranks decently in all factors contributing to economic development, rather than neglecting one factor at the expense of scoring highly in another.

Antithesis 2: Reducing income inequality hinders economic development, as it may slow economic growth.

1. Redistribution of wealth via progressive taxation or other means may cause an increased substitution effect. This is a phenomenon where high income

earners become disincentivised from working longer hours, since wages earned per additional hour would simply be subjected to a higher marginal tax rate. Furthermore, in countries where generous welfare benefits are given to lower income earners to reduce income inequality, there may be less of an incentive to work, as their basic necessities have already been taken care of. This would cause a decrease in economic output as workers choose to become underutilised and work shorter hours; real national income falls.

2. There may also be an increased possibility of brain drain - the emigration of highly-trained or qualified workers to countries with lower taxes, in order to enjoy a higher purchasing power and material SOL. In 2012, there was an intensification in the exodus of highly-skilled New Zealanders to Australia, with New Zealand's push factor being its substantially higher tax rates. Such brain drain would lead to a decrease in quantity and quality of the skilled workforce causing a fall in the full employment output of the economy, as well as a decrease in consumer spending. There would be both a fall in the Long Run Aggregate Supply and Aggregate Demand respectively, causing a fall in economic growth, ceteris paribus.

3. Lastly, the government incurs an opportunity cost, or the next best alternative forgone, when pursuing income redistribution by using its tax revenue to fund the direct provision of or subsidise merit goods. For instance, the government may have had to forgo building more transport infrastructure, which could potentially also increase the standard of living of all residents by increasing the level of efficiency of the public transport system.

<u>Concluding Section</u>

1. Empirically, a reduction in income inequality does seem to improve the economic development of a country. However, while it is likely more helpful than harmful, it is alone not sufficient to ensure progress in development. As there are many other factors to take into account, government policies needed to improve economic development go far beyond reducing the income gap and should include policies to deliberately boost the training and education opportunities for the lower income.

2. Critically, efforts to reduce income inequality should not inadvertently retard economic growth. Thus, the degree of progressivity of the income tax system and extent of government handouts also need to be carefully calibrated.

9. Explain the consequences of an import quota. (10)

Introduction

1. An import quota is a restriction placed on the quantity of imports allowed into the country.

2. This is a form of protectionism, which involves any attempt by a country to impose restrictions on the open trade in goods and services and mostly involves imposing trade barriers on imports in order to shield domestic industries from foreign competition.

3. Implementing an import quota will bring about consequences for the following stakeholders: domestic consumers, domestic producers, foreign producers, the government, and society as a whole.

Imposition of Import Quota

1. In 2019, the European Union (EU) imposed quotas on a variety of products, including imported steel shipments, in order to safeguard EU steel.

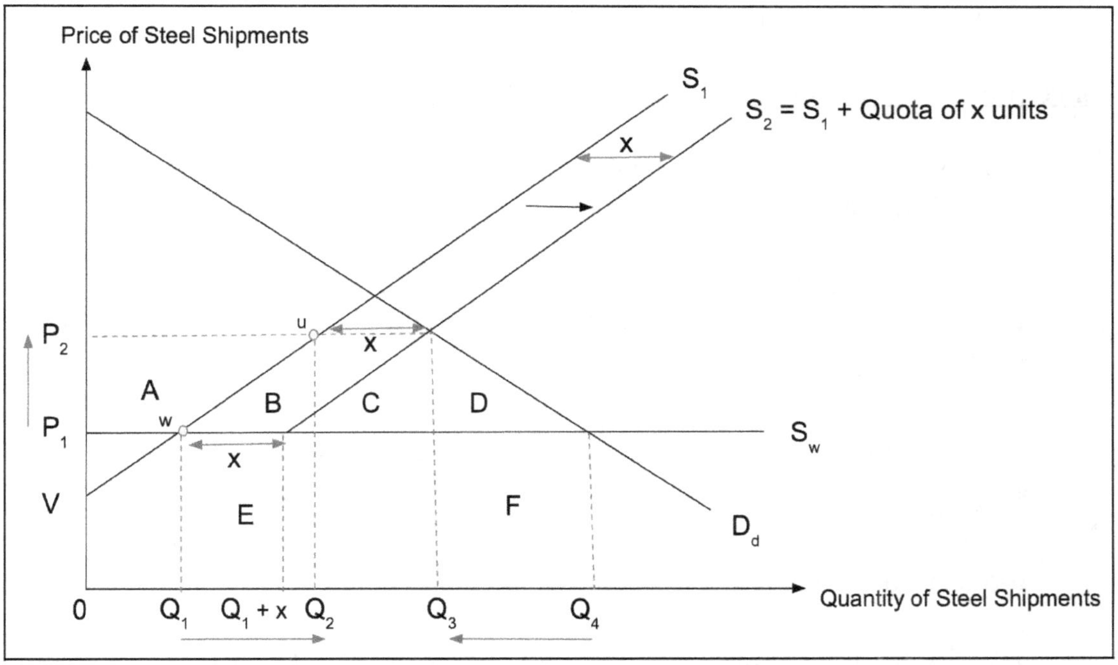

Fig 1: Imposing Quotas on Steel Shipments

2. Prior to the imposition of the quota, EU countries could purchase as many steel shipment imports as they wished at the price P_1, as shown by the horizontal, perfectly price elastic world supply curve, S_w.

3. At P_1, the quantity of steel shipments demanded was Q_4, quantity supplied by domestic producers was Q_1, and quantity imported was therefore Q_1Q_4.

4. Suppose a quota of x units was imposed by the EU; no more than x units of steel imports could be introduced into EU countries. The effective total supply within an EU country thus becomes $S_2 = S_1 + x\ units$, instead of S_w. However, the domestic supply curve has not changed and remains at S_1.

Consequences on Domestic Consumers

1. Domestic consumers usually 'lose out' following the imposition of such import quotas. Firstly, with the decreased available quantity in the country being the domestic supply plus no more than x units, the price of steel shipments in the domestic market rises from P_1 to P_2.

2. As a result of this price increase, domestic consumption of steel shipments decreases from Q_4 to Q_3 in accordance with the law of demand, which states that price and quantity demanded are inversely related, ceteris paribus.

3. Due to the increased price coupled with the decrease in consumption of steel shipments, there is a decrease in consumer surplus in the form of a loss in Areas A + B + C + D (trapezium).

Consequences on Domestic Producers and Workers

1. Domestic producers, on the other hand, typically 'gain' from the imposition of import quotas.

2. In accordance with the law of supply which states that an increase in price would lead to an increase in quantity supplied, domestic production increases from Q_1 to Q_2.

3. The increase in price and quantity transacted leads to an increase in revenue earned by domestic producers, from P_1Q_1 to P_2Q_2. Profits (total revenue minus total cost) should also increase assuming unit costs of production remain unchanged.

4. The domestic producer surplus also increases from VP_1w to VP_2u, by area A.

5. The increase in production from Q_1 to Q_2 implies that there is concurrently an increase in employment, as the hiring of workers (a derived-demand) increases.

Consequences on Foreign Producers

1. With foreign producers of steel shipments, it is ambiguous as to whether they 'gain' or 'lose out' following the imposition of the import quotas; this varies depending on the situation.

2. Assuming that the government issues import licences to foreign producers, rectangular area C or $Q_2Q_3 \times P_2$ is generally pocketed by foreign firms, adding to the firms' revenue.

3. However, there is a fall in imported quantity from Q_1Q_4 to Q_2Q_3. The revenue has decreased by the amount equivalent to the summation of Areas E or $Q_1Q_2 \times P_1$, as well as Area F or $Q_3Q_4 \times P_1$.

4. Hence, whether foreign producers gain or lose out is dependent on whether the magnitude of the loss of Areas E and F (due to a fall in import quantity) is greater than, less than, or equal to that of the gain in Area C (due to an increase in price).

5. Should Areas E and F be greater than Area C, foreign producers would 'lose out' due to the loss in revenue and, ceteris paribus, profits. On the other hand, if Areas E and F are smaller than Area C, the foreign producers would 'gain' due to the increase in revenue and, ceteris paribus, profits.

Consequences on Society

1. Society is said to 'lose out' overall.

2. Considering all stakeholders, there is a net welfare loss of Areas B + D. If only the domestic economy is considered, there is a deadweight welfare loss of Areas B + C + D.

3. The welfare loss of Area D is caused by the fall in consumption of steel shipments by Q_4Q_3; consumer surplus equivalent to Area D has now dissipated because of the quota.

4. The welfare loss of Area B is due to productive inefficiency caused by the extra cost paid as the economy shifts purchases from efficient overseas firms to inefficient domestic firms for the quantity of Q_1Q_2. Previously, the production cost by foreign firms to produce Q_1Q_2 units was only Area E; with the import quota, the cost (now shouldered by inefficient domestic firms) increased to Areas B + E.

5. Consumer surplus equivalent to Area C has also dissipated due to the higher price, adding to the welfare loss to the domestic economy.

10. Discuss if central banks should choose to target exchange rates to achieve economic growth and price stability, instead of interest rates. (15)

Introduction

1. The central bank has various roles, including but not limited to: regulating the money supply, carrying out monetary policies, executing exchange rate policies, and being the holder of foreign exchange reserves in the economy.

2. The exchange rate refers to the price of a country's currency in terms of foreign currency. When the government manipulates exchange rates, depending on whether the economy uses a fixed or managed-float exchange rate system, there could be either a devaluation or revaluation (fixed exchange rate system), depreciation or appreciation (managed-float system) of the currency.

3. A devaluation or depreciation occurs when the value of a country's currency decreases in relation to foreign currency in a fixed exchange rate system or floating exchange rate system respectively.

4. In contrast, a revaluation or appreciation occurs when the value of a country's currency increases in relation to foreign currency in a fixed exchange rate system or floating exchange rate system respectively.

5. Interest rates refer to payment for borrowed money over a certain time period, expressed as a percentage of the borrowed amount. Interest rates also refer to the rate of return on savings.

Exchange Rate Policy Thesis 1: Depreciation brings about economic growth.

1. Economic growth can refer to actual and/or potential economic growth.

2. Actual economic growth occurs when there is an increase in the real Gross Domestic Product (GDP) of the economy, usually over a year.

3. Potential economic growth occurs when there is an increase in the economy's capacity to produce at full employment, operating at the given level of technology with all factors of production fully and efficiently utilised. The level of potential output has increased.

4. $Aggregate\ Demand\ (AD) = (C) + (G) + (I) + (X - M)$. Since (X-M) is a component of AD, an increase in the value of net exports (X-M) would enable an increase in economic growth. This can be achieved via increasing export revenue and/or decreasing import expenditure.

5. During his term, President Trump advocated for depreciating the United States Dollar (USD) against other major currencies, reasoning that a weaker dollar would increase USA export revenue and decrease their import expenditure.

6. This is because when the value of USD falls in relation to other currencies, USA exports would be cheaper in terms of foreign currency and foreigners would increase their demand for USA goods, increasing export revenue earned (X).

7. The depreciation of the USD would also cause imports from other countries to become more expensive in terms of domestic currency. This leads to consumers making the switch from more expensive imports to domestically-produced goods and services, decreasing the quantity demanded for imports and import expenditure (M), and increasing domestic consumption (C).

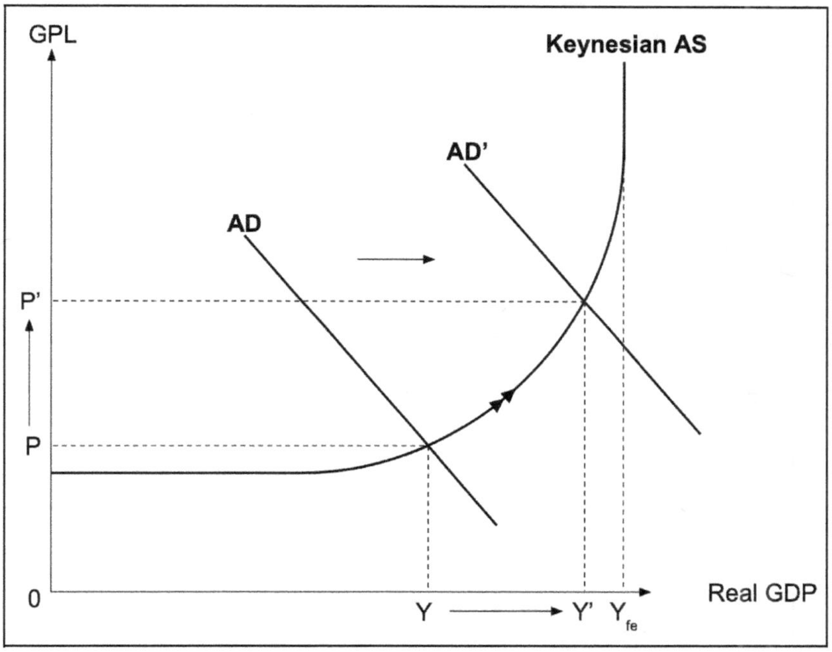

Fig 1: Increase in AD

8. With an increase in (X) and a decrease in (M), (X-M) would increase. Coupled with a rise in (C), AD would shift rightward from *AD* to *AD'*, increasing real GDP from *Y* to *Y'*, enabling economic growth to be achieved.

Exchange Rate Policy Thesis 2: Appreciation is useful for tackling high inflation.

1. Inflation refers to the sustained increase in the General Price Level (GPL) of an economy over a given time period. Price stability means low and steady inflation.

2. This contrasts with deflation, like in the case of Japan's "Two Lost Decades", or high and excessive inflation, the most extreme of which is hyperinflation like in the case of Zimbabwe.

3. An appreciation in the domestic currency would cause exports to become more expensive in terms of foreign currency, decreasing the demand for these exports and hence decreasing (X).

4. In contrast, imports become cheaper in terms of domestic currency. This leads to consumers making the switch from domestically-produced to relatively cheaper imported goods, increasing imports instead and decreasing (C).

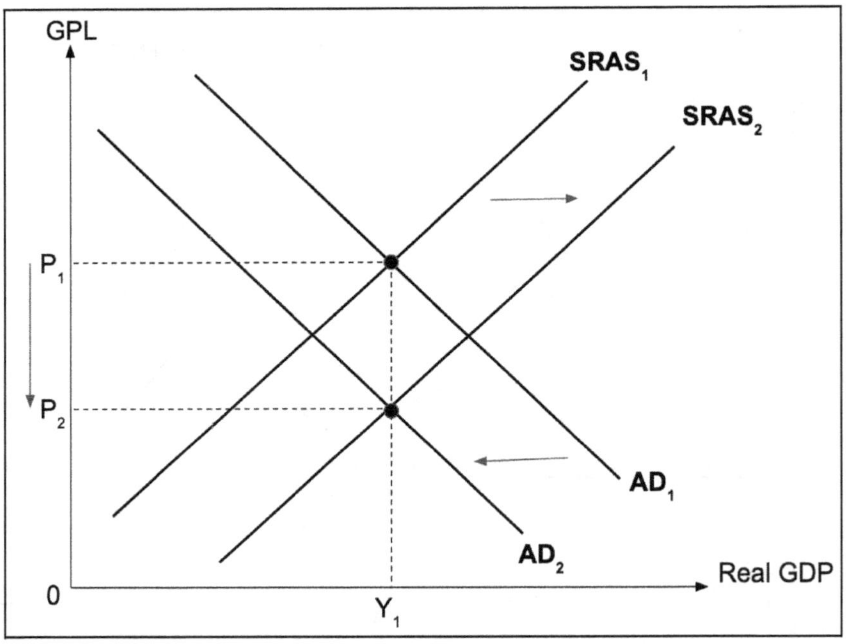

Fig 2: Fall in AD and Increase in SRAS due to Currency Appreciation

5. With a decrease in (X) and increase in (M), the value of (X-M) falls. Coupled with a fall in (C), AD would decrease and shift leftwards from AD_1 to AD_2.

6. Simultaneously, with access to cheaper imports in terms of domestic currency, factors of production can be obtained more cheaply, causing the unit costs of production for domestic goods and services to fall. This shifts the Short Run Aggregate Supply (SRAS) rightward from $SRAS_1$ to $SRAS_2$.

7. The combined effect of a leftward shift in AD and a rightward shift in SRAS enables the level of inflation to fall as the GPL decreases from from P_1 to P_2.

Monetary Policy Thesis 1: Monetary policy brings about economic growth.

1. Enacting a monetary policy refers to a conscious attempt by the central bank to influence the level of economic activity in an economy by changing the money supply and/or interest rates.

2. Expansionary monetary policy entails increasing the money supply and lowering interest rates in the economy. This would lower the cost of borrowing; households would be more willing and able to borrow from financial institutions especially to finance the purchase of big ticket items. They would also be less willing to save given the lower returns on savings, and thus more willing to spend instead. This would increase the level of (C).

3. Firms will also be more willing to borrow to finance investment projects, given that the lower interest rates will result in more investment projects being profitable. This will cause the level of (I) in the economy to increase. Referring back to Fig 1, together with the increase in (C), this would result in the same effect with AD shifting rightward from *AD* to *AD'*, increasing the real GDP from *Y* to *Y'*, enabling economic growth to be achieved.

4. In addition, with the increase in the level of (I), the accumulation of capital stock in the economy increases, allowing its productive capacity to increase, and potential growth to be achieved as well.

5. For example, during the USA's financial crisis in 2008, the Federal Reserve reduced interest rates to almost 0% to spur spending by consumers and firms.

Monetary Policy Thesis 2: Monetary policy brings about price stability.

1. Contractionary monetary policy results in a decrease in AD and could thus be used to bring about price stability, as the GPL would fall. This is achieved by decreasing the money supply and increasing interest rates with the effect of reducing (C) and (I).

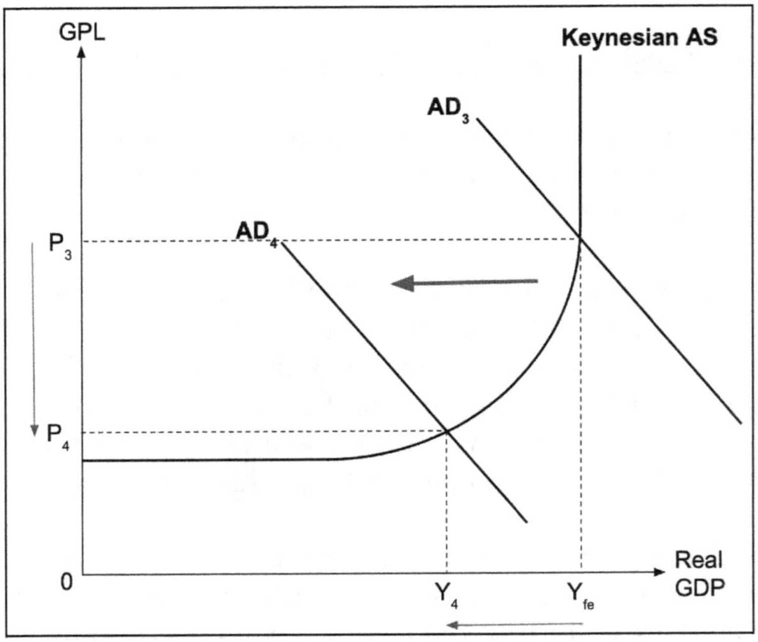

Fig 3: Fall in AD Due to Contractionary Monetary Policy

2. Referring to Fig 3, this would cause the AD to shift leftwards from AD_3 to AD_4, enabling the GPL to fall from P_3 to P_4. As a result, inflation is curbed.

<u>Exchange Rate Policy over Monetary Policy Reason 1: Some countries may not have the ability to implement (further) monetary policies.</u>

1. Spurring economic growth via an expansionary monetary policy may not be feasible for economies with already near-zero interest rates, like the USA from 2008 to 2015, and again in 2020 during the COVID pandemic.

2. Likewise, Japan had already pursued a policy of ultra-low or zero interest rates since 1999, and would likely be unable to implement further effective rounds of monetary policy.

3. Such economies are said to be stuck in a 'liquidity trap', where because interest rates are already near zero or zero, increasing the money supply further would fail to lower interest rates to stimulate the economy. In contrast, this issue does not occur with exchange rate policy.

<u>Exchange Rate Policy over Monetary Policy Reason 2: Exchange rate policies are likely more effective than monetary policies with regards to small and open economies.</u>

1. For small and open economies, the size of domestic demand would usually be much smaller compared to the size of foreigners' demand for their exports, the latter of which would normally be the main driver of the economy. For example, external demand accounts for about 75% of the AD for Singapore's goods.

2. In these cases, manipulating the exchange rates to increase foreign demand for exports, thus increasing the value of (X) and (X-M), would likely result in a much greater increase in real GDP compared to adjusting interest rates.

3. Furthermore, in small and open economies like Singapore, adjusting interest rates may not be an option, due to short term capital movements that would negate changes in the interest rates. For example, if the Monetary Authority of Singapore were to lower interest rates, large volumes of hot money outflows would occur as investors move their hot money investments elsewhere to receive higher returns. This would reduce the money supply in Singapore, raising interest rates back up. That is why Singapore, an interest rate taker, follows "world" interest rates, and does not attempt to manipulate its own.

<u>Exchange Rate Policy over Monetary Policy Reason 3: Exchange rate policies have a higher chance of being successful compared to monetary policies, as the former do not rely on domestic economic sentiments.</u>

1. Additionally, exchange rate policies would likely be more fruitful in stimulating economic growth compared to monetary policies, especially in cases where the domestic consumer and business sentiments are poor.

2. Should the domestic economic outlook be poor, despite decreasing interest rates, households may still be unwilling to take up loans for fear that they may be unable to repay them. Similarly, firms may still be unwilling to borrow to finance investment projects, given the uncertainty over the rate of return on such investments.

3. If this is the case, both (C) and (I) may not increase despite implementing the expansionary monetary policy, and economic growth may not be achieved.

4. It may thus be more effective to tap on foreign demand to increase (X) to stimulate economic growth.

<u>Exchange Rate Policy over Monetary Policy Reason 4: Monetary policies may be counterproductive to achieving economic growth.</u>

1. Implementing an expansionary monetary policy involves lowering interest rates which may lead to asset bubbles. This is because the borrowed funds could be used to finance the purchase of assets such as stocks and properties.

2. This may fuel speculative activity in the asset or property market and cause a housing bubble, for example. When such a bubble bursts, prices plunge, and households may default on large loans taken, resulting in bankruptcies.

3. An example of this was the failure of the Bank of Japan to tighten its monetary easing policy in time, leading to an uncontrolled money supply, overly-easy access to credit, an overheated economy and soaring asset prices. This fuelled

Japan's asset bubble from 1986 to 1991 where stock and real estate prices were highly inflated.

4. When the asset bubble burst in 1992, Japan's economic growth declined tremendously due to widespread bankruptcies and credit crunch. Long periods of deflation ensued, contributing to "Japan's Lost Decade". This continued for many years, to the extent that many call the last 20 years "Japan's Two Lost Decades".

<u>Monetary Policy over Exchange Rate Policy Reason 1: It is more feasible to adjust interest rates compared to exchange rates.</u>

1. One benefit of implementing monetary policies instead, is the ability of the central bank to fine-tune interest rates accordingly. Interest rates can be reviewed and changed incrementally, and are easier to control compared to exchange rates, as the latter could lead to a depletion in foreign exchange (FOREX) reserves which prevents further fine-tuning.

2. Frequent changes to exchange rates also result in uncertainties that will hinder trade and cross-border investments, which in turn can be worse for both economic growth and price stability.

3. Furthermore, adjusting exchange rates is more onerous, as there are many more factors affecting the demand and supply of currency in the FOREX market, including currency speculators.

<u>Monetary Policy over Exchange Rate Policy Reason 2: Interest rate policies can also influence exchange rates, thus "killing two birds with one stone".</u>

1. Interest rate policies can also indirectly influence exchange rates and bring about the benefits of currency appreciation or depreciation as well. Hence, using interest rate policies would be like 'killing two birds with one stone'.

2. A fall in interest rates would cause a decrease in hot money flows into the economy, as well as an increase in hot money flows out of the economy. This is because investors would choose to shift their funds to other countries whose interest rates are higher to gain greater returns on their savings. In order to do this, investors would need to sell domestic currency in the FOREX market to buy foreign currency instead, thereby increasing the supply of domestic currency. With a surplus in domestic currency, ceteris paribus, the exchange rate would depreciate.

3. Hence, both the benefits of a falling interest rate and depreciating exchange rate, can be experienced at the same time. The same principle applies for increasing interest rates, as the exchange rate would appreciate simultaneously.

4. However, it must be noted that this indirect effect only happens if the economy is open to short-term capital flows.

<u>Monetary Policy over Exchange Rate Policy Reason 3: Depreciation may cause retaliation, leading to a deterioration in economic growth instead.</u>

1. Countries may come under fire for keeping their exchange rates artificially low, and may be labelled as 'currency manipulators'. This is because a rise in the net exports of the domestic country may mean a fall for others, and by extension, lower economic growth and higher unemployment for other countries.

2. This may spark competitive devaluation whereby foreign countries likewise depreciate their respective currencies in a tit-for-tat manner. If this arises, any initial economic boost for the domestic country would only be temporary. With adverse international relations, trade and economic growth for all countries involved may spiral downwards instead.

<u>Monetary Policy over Exchange Rate Policy Reason 4: Monetary policies would be more successful than exchange rate policies in domestic demand-oriented economies.</u>

1. Should the economy not be export-reliant, but rather, rely more heavily on domestic demand to drive economic growth, then the depreciation of a currency may not have as large an impact on economic growth. Though (M) may still decrease, without as large an increase in (X), the effect on (X-M) and by extension, real GDP, may not be that significant.

2. For instance, in 2020, Indonesia's "exports of goods and services" as a percentage of GDP was only about 17%, whereas its domestic consumption as a percentage of GDP was about 60%.

3. Countries like Indonesia who rely more heavily on domestic demand may not be affected as much by exchange rate policies. On the other hand, as interest rates largely affect the domestic demand, economic growth can be achieved to a much greater extent.

<u>Monetary Policy over Exchange Rate Policy Reason 5: Currency depreciation to spur economic growth would adversely affect the price stability of import-dependent economies.</u>

1. If an economy relies heavily on imported final goods and factor inputs, an exchange rate policy would drastically increase the GPL, compared to the effect of inflation when using an expansionary monetary policy to spur economic growth. Japan is one such example, as its economy is highly dependent on imported oil as well as other commodities.

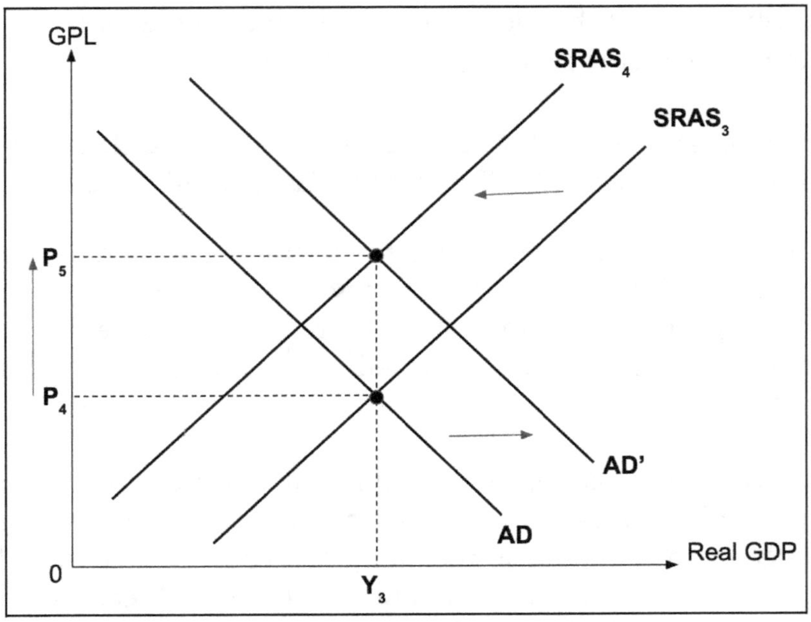

Fig 4: Increase in AD and Fall in SRAS due to Currency Depreciation

2. Depreciation would result in imported, cost-push inflation, given the relatively higher price of imports now, in terms of domestic currency. As the cost of factor inputs rise, the unit costs of production would increase, decreasing the SRAS and shifting it leftward from $SRAS_3$ to $SRAS_4$. Despite the increase in AD as previously explained in Fig 1, the fall in SRAS would counteract the expansionary objectives of the exchange rate policy and may offset the effects of a rising AD, causing the real GDP to be stagnant at Y_3 and instead causing the GPL to rise from P_4 to P_5.

3. Higher inflation would erode the purchasing power of residents, and they would be less willing and able to finance the purchase of necessities.

<u>Concluding Section</u>

1. At the end of the day, the policy that should be used is that which has the highest chance of success in stimulating economic growth and/or controlling price stability, while also having the least unintended adverse effects on the economy.

2. One critical factor would be the nature of the economy. For example, one that is highly reliant on exports as the main driver of economic growth would likely be better off employing an exchange rate policy. On the other hand, if the economy is more domestic demand-dependent, an interest rate policy could be more effective instead.

3. Other factors affecting the success of the policy could include the domestic economic outlook; this would largely affect the success of monetary policies, but not so much that of exchange rate policies, which may be more affected by

the state of foreign economies and how investors view any exchange rate changes.

4. The feasibility of each policy need also be considered; some countries may simply be unable to implement an expansionary monetary policy successfully if they are already stuck in a 'liquidity trap', for instance.

Note: This essay is lengthier than what would be needed for a 15 mark question. The front parts of this essay explaining how the policies work can be omitted. They are included here for purposes of revision and may answer a preceding 10m essay on how the policies work.

11. Explain the effects on relevant stakeholders when the government gives subsidies to domestic producers as a form of protectionism. (10)

Introduction

1. Protectionism involves any attempt by a country to impose restrictions on the open trade in goods and services, and mostly involves imposing trade barriers on imports in order to shield domestic industries from foreign competition.

2. A subsidy is a grant provided by the government to domestic firms with the aim of lowering production costs and increasing total output.

3. In wealthier countries, rice farmers earn a substantial proportion of their income (sometimes even as high as 75%) through protectionist measures like production subsidies, with global rice subsidies averaging $1 billion a year since 1998.

4. Some of the affected stakeholders include the domestic consumers, domestic producers, foreign producers, government and society.

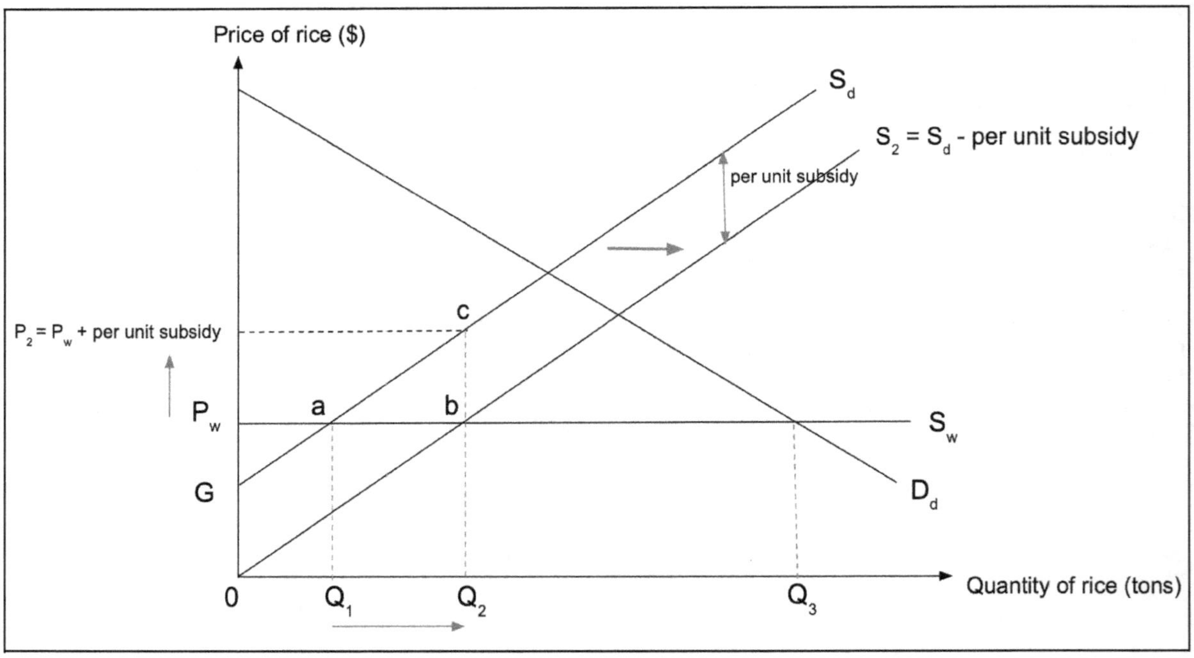

Fig 1: Imposition of Subsidy

Stakeholder 1: Effect on Domestic Producers and Workers

1. As the subsidy is aimed to protect domestic producers from foreign competition, domestic producers 'gain' from the per unit subsidy.

2. Prior to the subsidy given to domestic producers, the price of rice was P_w. This assumes a world supply curve that is perfectly price elastic at S_w. At this price, the quantity supplied by domestic producers was only Q_1.

3. With the subsidy, the domestic supply curve for rice shifts rightwards from S_d to S_2. Though outwardly the price of rice in the market remains at the world price P_w, that which is earned by domestic firms (inclusive of the per unit subsidy) increases to P_2.

4. Therefore, the quantity supplied by domestic producers increases to Q_2 as they are now more incentivised to produce a higher quantity in accordance with the law of supply, which states that price and quantity supplied are directly related.

5. There is an increase in revenue earned from $P_w \times Q_1$ to $P_2 \times Q_2$. Ceteris paribus, domestic producers are thus expected to earn higher profits as well, since profits are the difference between total revenue and total costs.

6. There is also an increase in producer surplus due to the increased quantity transacted and higher "after subsidy" price, of area P_wP_2ca.

7. Furthermore, the increase in production from Q_1 to Q_2 implies an increase in employment; more workers (a derived-demand) would be employed in the rice industry, which can reduce the unemployment rate in the economy.

<u>Stakeholder 2: Effect on Domestic Consumers</u>

1. Domestic consumers are unaffected, as the quantity of rice consumed before and after the subsidy remains unchanged at Q_3, as the price of rice remains unchanged at P_w as well.

<u>Stakeholder 3: Effect on Foreign Producers</u>

1. Foreign producers are said to 'lose out'. Prior to domestic producers receiving subsidies, the quantity of rice imported from foreign producers is Q_1Q_3. Now, the quantity of rice imported from foreign producers falls to Q_2Q_3.

2. Hence, there is a decrease in revenue earned by foreign producers, from $(Q_1Q_3)P_w$ to $(Q_2Q_3)P_w$ instead. Consequently, profits are expected to fall as well.

Stakeholder 4: Government

1. The government is said to 'lose out', given the total subsidy expense equal to P_wP_2cb that is incurred. This also incurs an opportunity cost in terms of the next best alternative forgone; government revenue spent on subsidies may come at the expense of funding other merit goods like healthcare, or public goods like the building of anti-flood measures.

2. However, the Government will likely gain greater political support from domestic producers and workers.

Stakeholder 5: Society

1. Society incurs a welfare loss of triangle abc. This is due to productive inefficiency stemming from the extra cost paid as the economy shifts from purchasing rice from efficient overseas firms, to less efficient domestic firms for the quantity Q_1Q_2. The total cost to produce Q_1Q_2 units of rice by domestic firms is equal to triangle Q_1Q_2ca, whereas the same quantity was originally produced by the more efficient overseas firms at area Q_1Q_2ba.

2. In addition, due to opportunity costs incurred from the government spending, further welfare losses may be incurred if there is less provision of merit and public goods.

12. Using real world examples, explain possible causes of a deterioration in the Financial Account of the Balance of Payments. (10)

Introduction

1. The Balance of Payments (BOP) is a record of all economic transactions taking place between residents of a domestic country and of other countries, usually over a year, showing all payments received from other countries (inflows or credit) and all payments made to other countries (outflows or debit).

2. The Financial Account is the net inflow or outflow of funds for transactions in financial and physical assets, comprising Foreign Direct Investments (FDIs), Portfolio Investments and changes in Official Reserve Assets.

3. A deterioration in the Financial Account occurs when there are increasing net outflows out of, or falling net inflows into, the account.

Possible Cause 1: Poor Economic Outlook Affecting FDIs into the Country

1. FDIs are long-term fixed investments on capital goods, and are usually carried out by multinational corporations (MNCs). Such MNCs usually choose the countries in which they engage in FDI based on factors like economic outlook. If there are poor business sentiments about an economy, then MNCs would be less willing to invest in the country.

2. In 2021, FDIs in Myanmar fell to an eight year low following political unrest caused by the military takeover amidst the COVID pandemic. Given the uncertainty over the political future and public safety in the country, business investments were deemed 'high risks', leading to lower expected rate of returns and profits on investment projects. This resulted in a fall in the level of FDI inflows into Myanmar.

Possible Cause 2: Increase in Direct Investments Abroad by Domestic Firms

1. Should domestic firms grow successfully and possess the financial resources to expand into foreign markets, domestic firms may conduct outward Direct Investments in foreign countries in order to penetrate new foreign markets to diversify their revenue streams, increase their revenue, and by extension, their profits.

2. Furthermore, with a larger scale of production due to output produced in various countries, greater internal economies of scale can be reaped by these

firms, lowering the per unit cost of production and increasing profits, which is the difference between revenue and costs.

3. Another potential reason for firms conducting Direct Investments Abroad may be the rising costs of production in their domestic country, leading both local and foreign firms to relocate their production to other more cost-competitive economies. This is because rising costs of production back home would eat into their profit margin, reducing profitability. By relocating, their unit cost of production is lowered, increasing their profits.

4. These Direct Investments Abroad would cause an increase in outflows from the Financial Account. Coupled with a fall in inward FDIs due to higher costs of production, there would be a deterioration in the Financial Account.

5. From 2010 - 2020, Japanese firms moved away from export-oriented domestic production, and instead have shifted their focus to FDIs or FDI-driven overseas production. In 2013, net outward Direct Investments rose to 13 trillion yen, registering the second highest figure in Japan since 1985. This, amongst other reasons, likely accounted for Japan's Financial Account deficit of US $4.25 billion in 2013.

6. From 2019 to 2021, the USA was the leading country in the world for FDI outflows. In 2021, its FDI outflows totalled US $9,814 billion (for comparison, China ranked second globally for FDI outflows at US $2,581 billion). This, amongst other reasons, contributed to the USA's Financial Account deficit in 2021.

Possible Cause 3: Fall in Relative Interest Rates Affecting Portfolio Investments

1. Interest rates refer to payment for borrowed money over a certain time period, expressed as a percentage of the borrowed amount. Interest rates also refer to the rate of return on savings, as established by the financial institutions whose services are used.

2. Portfolio Investments can be short term or long term. Long term Portfolio Investments usually refer to the purchase of shares and government bonds, while short term portfolio investments refer mainly to hot money investments.

3. Hot money flows are short term monetary flows that move in and out of markets quickly, due to currency speculation or in seek of higher interest rates.

4. In this case, the country with relatively lower interest rates, either due to a fall in domestic interest rates or a rise in foreign interest rates, may face hot money outflows. This is because lower relative interest rates would result in lower expected rates of return on Portfolio Investments; investors would likely rather withdraw their investments and redirect their investments to countries with relatively higher interest rates and hence, expected rates of return.

5. The country experiencing hot money outflows may also face a fall in hot money inflows as fewer investors want to start engaging in Portfolio Investments in such a country. Ceteris paribus, this combined effect of an increase in hot money outflows, and decrease in hot money inflows, would cause a deterioration in its Financial Account.

6. For example, in June 2022, the Federal Reserve enacted the "most aggressive interest rate hike since 1994", raising the federal funds rate (target interest rate) by 0.75%. That led to major concerns in China as well as that this would "drive away hot money from China", increasing hot money outflows from China and instead increasing inflows into the USA, as the USA's interest rate hike came amidst China's monetary easing policy (lowering interest rates). If this were to continue to happen, China's Financial Account may be adversely affected like what contributed to the 1995 Mexican Peso Crisis.

13. Using real world examples, explain why governments may pursue free trade agreements. (10)

Introduction

1. A free trade agreement (FTA) refers to a legal commitment between countries to reduce trade barriers between them, while allowing each country to retain the right to pursue its own trade policy towards non-member countries.

2. Examples of this include the North American Free Trade Area (NAFTA) established in 1994, comprising America, Canada and Mexico. This has since been superseded by the United States-Mexico-Canada Agreement (USMCA) or "NAFTA 2.0" in 2020 - a modernised version of NAFTA accounting for intellectual property and digital trade.

3. Other examples of FTAs include the bilateral Australia-China Free Trade Agreement which came into force in 2015, the Pacific Alliance-Singapore Free Trade Agreement (PASFTA) since 2022 comprising Singapore and four members of the Pacific Alliance: Chile, Colombia, Mexico and Peru.

4. Governments pursue such trade agreements to achieve the macroeconomic goals of a country: sustainable economic growth, low unemployment, low and steady inflation, and a favourable Balance of Payments (BOP).

5. The fulfilment of the macroeconomic objectives as a result of pursuing FTAs can be attributed to three main reasons: an expansion of production into larger markets, an increased level of efficiency and innovation, and an increased level of investments in the economy.

Reason 1: Expansion into New Markets

1. With FTAs, comes the increased ability for domestic producers to expand their consumer base beyond their national boundaries, in new markets - the FTA partner countries.

2. As demand for a country's exports increases due to the expansion into new markets, export revenue (X) increases as well. This would enable net exports (X-M) to rise, increasing Aggregate Demand (AD) thus boosting economic growth.

3. From 1993 to 2015, under NAFTA, the total trilateral merchandise trade between the USA, Mexico and Canada had more than tripled. Trade volume between the USA and Canada experienced a 160% increase, while that of USA-Mexico faced a 465% increase, and that of Mexico-Canada faced a 750% increase over the same period.

4. Hence, from 1993 to 2016, USA exports soared. During this period, USA exports to Mexico and Canada rose 156%, contrasting with the 65% increase in USA exports to the rest of the world. Some have said that NAFTA boosted USA economic growth by as much as 0.5% a year, with the agricultural, automobile and service industries benefitting the most.

Reason 2: Increased Efficiency and Innovation

1. The reduction in trade barriers causes a greater quantity of imports to enter the domestic market, forcing domestic producers to compete with lower cost producers from FTA partner countries.

2. This incentivises domestic producers to undertake research and development (R&D) activities, increasing the level of process and product innovation in the country so as to make their products more price and non-price competitive, and be able to compete with foreign producers.

3. As more efficient methods of production arise, unit costs of production would fall, making domestic goods more price-competitive. With a lower price, in accordance with the law of demand which states that price and quantity demanded are inversely related, the quantity demanded of domestic goods will increase. Product innovation would also lead to improvements in the quality and reliability of a country's goods, enabling the demand for domestic goods to increase.

4. This would enable the country's domestic consumption (C) to increase, as consumers switch from purchasing imports to their own domestic goods. The domestic country's export earnings (X) would rise as well, as the demand for its exports increases.

5. A report in 2002 by López-Córdova estimated that the "whole package of NAFTA-related phenomena, namely lower Mexican tariffs, the preferential tariff margin in the USA...and participation of foreign producers" had increased the total factor productivity (an indicator measuring innovation performance) in Mexico by 10%.

6. Hence, process and product innovation would increase the competitiveness of the economy as a whole, increasing its level of (C) and (X-M), ceteris paribus. As both of these are components of AD, actual economic growth is achieved.

7. Furthermore, potential growth is achieved as well, since innovation often involves technological advancements and the accumulation of capital stock in the economy.

Reason 3: Increased Investments

1. The enlarged export market as a result of the FTA would likely give rise to increased investment, including that of Foreign Direct Investments (FDIs) by multinational corporations (MNCs). This is because firms would likely want to take advantage of the preferential access into FTA partner markets. These investments may be initiated by firms from FTA-partner countries and even non-FTA countries.

2. There would be an increase in the level of (I) in the economy. Due to an increase in the level of (I), the accumulation of capital stock in the economy would also increase, increasing the productive capacity of the economy.

3. As these firms are export-focused, they will also help increase the quantity of exports and export revenue (X). Ceteris paribus, (X-M) will increase.

Combined Effects of Reasons 1, 2, 3: Fulfilment of Macroeconomic Objectives - Economic Growth, Decreasing Unemployment, Improving BOP.

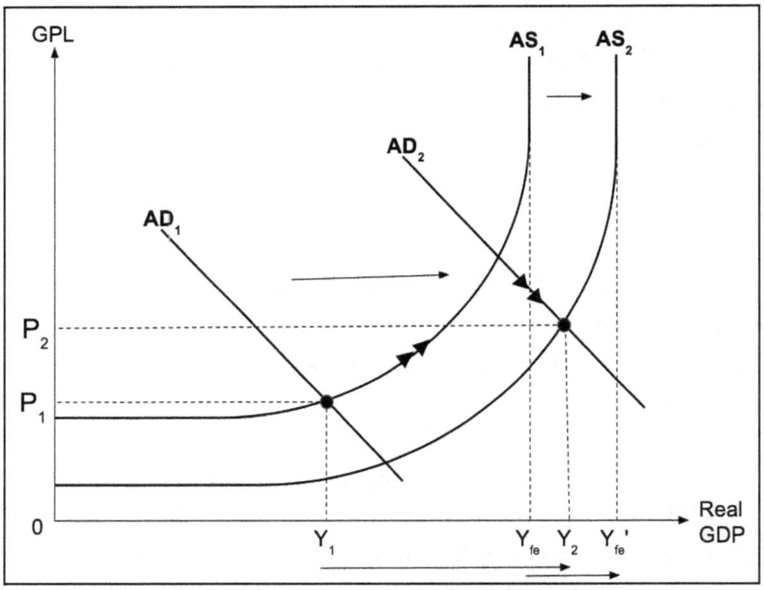

Fig 1: Actual and Potential Growth

1. The combined effect of the increased (C), (I) and (X-M) as explained in Reasons 1, 2 and 3, causes the AD to shift rightward from AD_1 to AD_2, while the AS curve also shifts rightward from AS_1 to AS_2 due to an increase in (I) and technological advancement.

2. Due to the increase in AD, actual economic growth is achieved. As the full employment output increases from Y_{fe} to Y_{fe}', potential growth is spurred as well. The combined increases in the AD and AS would enable the real GDP to

increase from Y_1 where AD_1 and AS_1 previously intersected, to Y_2 where AD_2 and AS_2 now intersect.

3. Besides achieving both actual and potential economic growth, there are other positive effects on the employment rates, Current Account and Financial Account.

4. With an increase in AD, there is a decrease in unemployment, as more jobs for workers (a derived-demand) are created as well. One of the reasons why USA President Bill Clinton signed NAFTA in 1993 was his belief that the trade deal would "[mean] jobs. American jobs, and good paying American jobs." From 1993 to 2017, the unemployment rate in the country fell from 6.5% to 4.1%.

5. With an increase in (X-M), the Balance of Trade (BOT) improves as well and by extension, the Current Account, since the BOT is empirically the largest component of the Current Account.

6. With an increase in Foreign Direct Investments, the Financial Account would also improve due to the increased capital flows into the country. With improvements in both the Current and Financial Accounts, the country can achieve a more favourable BOP.

7. Hence, the ability of FTAs to help achieve the aforementioned macroeconomic goals and bring multiple benefits to the economy, would be reasons why governments pursue FTAs.

<u>*BONUS Reason 4: Trade Creation, enabling Fulfilment of Macroeconomic Objective - Greater Price Stability, as well as Net Gain in Societal Welfare.</u>

1. Trade creation occurs when countries that have signed an FTA, or are in a trading bloc, undergo greater specialisation according to Comparative Advantage, thereby causing a shift in production from higher cost domestic producers to lower cost sources within the trading bloc. The goods can now be obtained more cheaply from other members of the trading bloc.

2. For example, Mexico is known to have a Comparative Advantage in the production of fresh fruits and vegetables during certain times of the year, when USA farmers are not able to harvest produce due to the climatic conditions. Mexico's Comparative Advantage largely arises from its good climate, enabling commodities like avocados to be produced all-year round.

3. Suppose that, prior to the formation of NAFTA in 1994, the USA had placed a tariff on Mexican fresh produce. After NAFTA was established, the USA would remove the tariff (t) on Mexican fresh produce.

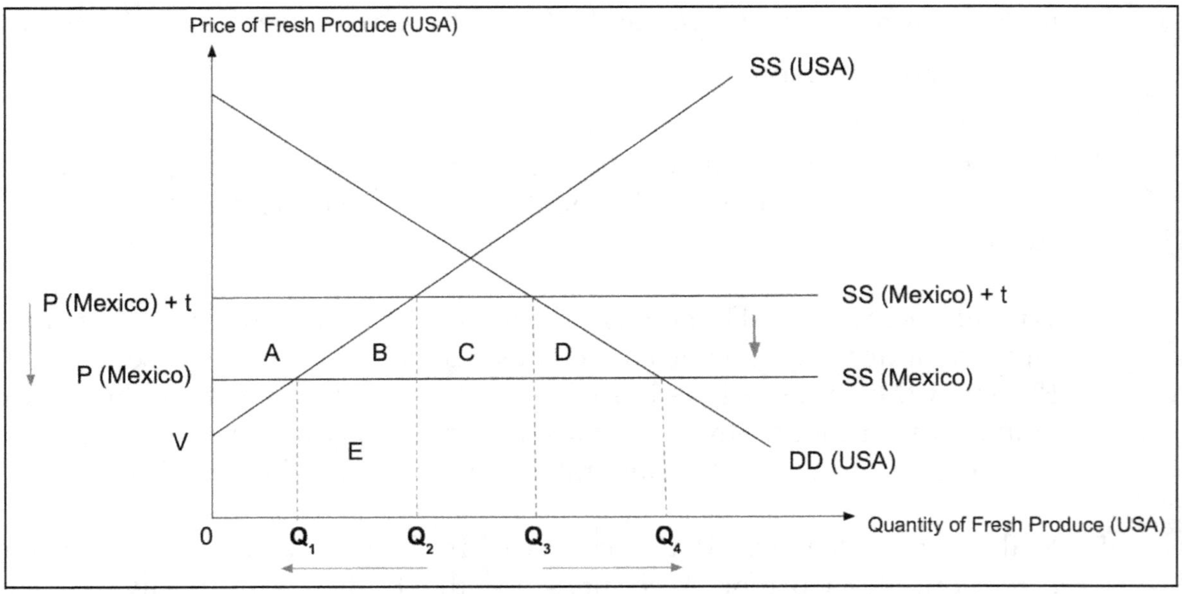

Fig 2: Removal of US Tariff on Mexican Fresh Produce following NAFTA

4. Assuming that trade occurs between the USA and Mexico only, referring to Fig 2, prior to NAFTA, the supply of Mexican fresh produce is represented by $SS\ (Mexico) + t$.

5. At this perfectly price elastic supply as denoted by the horizontal curve, the price paid per unit of fresh produce is equivalent to $P\ (Mexico) + t$. At this price, US quantity demanded for fresh produce is represented by Q_3, where $SS\ (Mexico) + t$ intersects $DD\ (USA)$.

6. At this price, USA producers would produce Q_2 units of fresh produce. In order to fulfil the excess demand, the USA would import Q_2Q_3 units of fresh produce from Mexico. However, with the formation of NAFTA, the tariffs on fresh produce would be removed.

7. The supply of Mexican fresh produce would be newly represented by $SS\ (Mexico)$, and the price of fresh produce would decrease to $P\ (Mexico)$. At this decreased price, in accordance with the law of demand which states that price and quantity demanded are inversely related, quantity demanded of fresh produce by the USA would increase from Q_3 to Q_4.

8. At this lower price, in accordance with the law of supply which states that price and quantity supplied are directly related, the USA would produce fewer units of fresh produce at Q_1, and import Q_1Q_4 units of produce from Mexico, the latter of which is greater than the imported quantity from before, Q_2Q_3.

9. Consumers would benefit from consuming more units of fresh produce (Q_4 units instead of Q_3 previously) at a lower price $P\,(Mexico)$ instead of $P\,(Mexico + t)$ previously. With lowered prices of such goods, inflation is lessened.

10. Should such imports be used as factors of production, the unit costs of production would be lowered as well. Ceteris paribus, cost savings may be transferred to consumers, enabling the GPL in the economy to be lower.

11. Though USA producers who are less efficient in production would suffer from the loss in producer surplus of Area A, and the USA government would also lose out due to the net loss of tax revenue represented by Area C, there is an overall net gain in societal welfare, represented by Area B + D.

12. The net gain in Area D is due to the increase in quantity of fresh produce consumed by Americans, while that of Area B is due to the lowered per unit price of fresh produce, as production shifts from inefficient domestic USA firms to foreign Mexican firms. Where previously the cost of producing Q_1Q_2 units were carried out by the inefficient domestic firms for the cost of Area B + E, it can now be carried out by more efficient Mexican firms for the cost of Area E.

13. This is also a two-way process; prior to the formation of NAFTA, USA exports to Mexico were heavily taxed as well, with tariffs of 30% or higher. In fact, Mexican tariffs on USA-made goods were, on average, 250% higher than USA tariffs on Mexican products. Thus, with NAFTA, Mexico would also import many more USA made goods at a much cheaper price, controlling inflation and increasing its societal welfare.

Note: The term "Free Trade Agreement" is not to be mixed up with "Free Trade Area". Member countries in a Free Trade Area may have signed free trade agreements, but countries who sign free trade agreements may not necessarily become a Free Trade Area. With free trade agreements, trade barriers are reduced but not necessarily eliminated.

14. Using real world examples, explain how the pursuit of economic integration may result in greater structural unemployment and income inequality. (10)

Introduction

1. Economic integration refers to economic cooperation between countries through coordinating economic policies, causing greater economic links to form between them.

2. Common examples of economic integration include Preferential Trade Agreements and the formation of trading blocs like a Free Trade Area, Customs Union, Common Market and Monetary Union.

3. The pursuit of economic integration typically results in the removal of most or all trade barriers between cooperating countries to allow freer trade to occur. Trade barriers are a form of protectionism; protectionism involves any attempt by a country to impose restrictions on the open trade in goods and services, and mostly involves imposing barriers on imports in order to shield domestic industries from foreign competition. Forms of protectionism include placing tariffs or quotas on imports and subsidising local producers.

4. In addition, there are types of economic integration that allow for free movement of factors of production. These adjustments often result in trade-offs that have to be made; these could lead to greater structural unemployment and income inequality.

5. Structural unemployment occurs when there is a mismatch between skills demanded by employers, and the skills which workers possess.

6. Income inequality refers to a situation in which there is an 'unfair' distribution of income across the population, with a large percentage of the national income being concentrated in the hands of the top few earners, while only a small percentage is earned by the majority.

Reason 1: Structural Unemployment and Income Inequality Result From Removal of Import Tariffs

1. A tariff is a tax placed on imported goods or services as a form of protectionism.

2. Prior to the signing of the North American Free Trade Agreement (NAFTA) and creation of the Free Trade Area comprising the USA, Canada and Mexico in 1994, the USA and Mexico imposed tariffs on each others' imports. After

economic integration occurred and NAFTA was established, these tariffs were mostly removed.

3. As Mexico possesses a Comparative Advantage in labour-intensive manufacturing goods, the lifting of import tariffs for certain manufactured goods resulted in the decline of such industries in the USA. Producing less output, firms retrenched workers who are no longer needed, given that workers are a derived-demand.

4. According to a 2011 study by the Economic Policy Institute, 61% of the net job losses (equivalent to 415,000 jobs) due to trade with Mexico under NAFTA, were "manufacturing jobs". This caused workers in specific USA states with an emphasis on manufacturing, namely California, Pennsylvania, Ohio, Indiana and Michigan, to suffer large job losses.

5. Although many job vacancies exist in industries in the Healthcare and Information Technology (IT) sector, many of the retrenched do not possess the technical skills needed to work in hospitals, or as IT analysts and software developers. They become structurally unemployed and many eventually take up lower-paying service jobs. Such widespread structural unemployment also results in a widening income gap.

<u>Reason 2: Structural Unemployment and Income Inequality Resulting from Factor Mobility</u>

1. In some forms of economic integration like the Common Market and Monetary Union, there is an added characteristic of being able to freely move factors of production across countries within the bloc, including labour.

2. Typically, higher-skilled workers are very limited in numbers to begin with, and they now face an even higher demand across the bloc. This contrasts with lower-skilled workers who are usually more in abundance, and now have to compete with many others across the bloc.

3. This would cause a phenomenon whereby many skilled workers across various cooperating countries would be able to easily find jobs and earn higher incomes, while many lower skilled workers will be left jobless, or given lower paying jobs than before due to fiercer job competition.

4. As these skilled workers are those who already earn higher-incomes in the first place, this phenomenon would foster income inequality; the rich get richer, while the poor get poorer.

5. This is one of the reasons why many British voted to leave the European Union (EU), a Common Market. Known as the "job factory of Europe", Britain had 2.1 million Europeans working in the country around the time of the referendum. Lower-skilled workers from economically less-developed countries like Turkey would flock to the UK in search of higher paying jobs.

6. Hence, Europeans were accused of "stealing jobs" in Britain and depressing local wages. With the increased supply of low-skilled workers, ceteris paribus, wages across the UK were lowered, as the Turkish were prepared to be hired for British jobs at lower wages than the British would previously accept.

7. In contrast, the white collar, higher income British workers were still able to keep their jobs and in some cases, earn even higher incomes than before. This is because numerous high income earners were firm or business owners who started to make higher profit margins due to lower-wage workers from other parts of the EU decreasing unit costs of production. Hence, due to income inequality that was reportedly exacerbated when Britain was in the EU, many voted to leave the EU during the Brexit referendum in 2016.

8. Besides labour, some forms of economic integration enable capital to be moved across borders. It was reported in 2014 that in Ohio, 14,653 USA jobs were attributed to being "directly lost due to NAFTA-related reasons like [the] relocation of USA firms to Mexico". A report in 2001 stated that in Pennsylvania, about 38,000 job losses could be attributed to "trade with Mexico and Canada". With lower income earners being retrenched as factories relocate to more cost-competitive economies, structural unemployment and income inequality rise as well.

15. Outline three of the Sustainable Development Goals. (10)

Introduction

1. The 17 Sustainable Development Goals (SDGs) are a set of indicators and their respective targets which the United Nations (UN) has pledged to achieve, in accordance with the "2030 Agenda for Sustainable Development".

2. These 17 SDGs were adopted by all UN member states in 2015, and serve as an immediate call to action for both developed and developing countries to embark on a worldwide partnership to tackle individual socioeconomic problems faced by many countries. This includes but is not limited to: poverty, health, education, inequality, other deprivations, a lack of economic growth, climate change and the preservation of wildlife.

3. It is hoped that achieving these goals would increase a country's economic development. Economic development refers to a sustained improvement in the standard of living of residents, comprising the material standard of living which is typically measured by the real national income per capita, as well as the non-material standard of living which is measured by indicators like the reduction in income inequality, better health and environmental standards, education, and employment opportunities.

SDG 1: No Poverty

1. This Goal is simply to "end poverty in all forms everywhere".

2. Since 2015, the World Bank has defined "extreme poverty" as individuals with an income below the international poverty line of "$1.90 a day", with the inability to fulfil basic human needs like having access to clean water and sanitation, education and health.

3. Target 1.1 of the Goal outlines the hope to eradicate extreme poverty everywhere, by 2030.

4. Unfortunately, COVID-19 pandemic has led to the first instance of an increase in extreme poverty in this generation, with about 120 million more individuals living in extreme poverty in 2020. Currently, more than 700 million people, or approximately 10% of the world's population, live in extreme poverty.

5. Thus, the UN is unlikely to fulfil its goal of ending poverty even if economies bounce back from the pandemic, though the UN is working towards it through the implementation of disaster risk reduction strategies and increasing the number of crucial services and social protection programmes available.

6. Target 1.2 outlines the goal of reducing the proportion of men, women and children of all ages living in poverty in all its various dimensions and respective national definitions, by at least half, by 2030. Different "respective national definitions" of poverty include, but are not limited to: "absolute poverty", "relative poverty", "persistent poverty", "situational poverty", "urban poverty", "rural poverty" and "generational poverty".

7. Target 1.3 suggests implementing national social protection systems and measures for all. Social protection measures are typically initiated by the government, and help the poor cope with crises and the loss of jobs, and ensure that they have adequate access to healthcare and education. Hence, by 2030, there should be substantial coverage for lower income earners.

<u>SDG 4: Quality Education</u>

1. This goal is to establish inclusive and equitable quality education, as well as encourage lifelong learning, for all.

2. Due to some lower income earners being unable to access education, it is difficult for them to gain upward social mobility. They are thus caught in a poverty trap, where incomes remain unchanged or even fall due to a lack of education and productivity. Hence, it is important to provide the lower income earners a means of gaining upward social mobility, usually through the direct provision of, or subsidising, education.

3. Over the last few decades, progress has been made to increase the overall literacy rates and education levels of the global population. Participation in organised pre-Primary educational activities increased from 65% in 2010 to 73% in 2019. Over the last 50 years, the adult global literacy rate rose from 67% in 1967 to 86% in 2019. School completion rates for Primary and Secondary school have risen by 3% and 7% in the last decade as well.

4. Despite this, according to the UN, there remains a "slow progress in school completion that is likely to get worse". Furthermore, despite students completing school courses, in 2020 alone for example, 101 million (9% of children) in Grades 1 to 8 were unable to perform at the minimum reading proficiency levels.

5. Hence, the targets laid out in this Goal spur countries to work towards boys and girls receiving equitable and quality education at the Primary and Secondary school level, with learning outcomes that will equip them with the necessary skills to find jobs in the future.

6. By 2030, it is also hoped that more youth and adults can access good technical, vocational and tertiary education. This will mean that more have specialised, niche skills which are in demand, decreasing the structural unemployment

rates in the country that originally stemmed from a skills mismatch between what employers demanded and what workers could supply.

SDG 5: Achieving Gender Equality and Empower All Women and Girls

1. Gender equality refers to the act of giving both males and females equal health, educational, economic, political and other opportunities.

2. Female empowerment refers to the elimination of discrimination faced by women and girls regarding access to education, healthcare, and in other spheres of social and economic life - for example, access to credit. It also includes the view of gender equality, where women and girls have access to equal opportunities as men and boys, achieving their potential to lead a fulfilling and productive life.

3. Women are severely under-represented in certain professional domains; in 2021, women only made up 25.6% of seats in national parliaments, 36.3% of representatives in local governments, and held only 28.2% of managerial positions. It is clear that in these domains, males heavily outnumber their female counterparts. In some cases, this is due to gender stereotypes and bias against women applying for these roles.

4. Hence, Target 5.1 highlights the importance of ending all types of discrimination against females in all places. Target 5.5 pledges to ensure women's full and effective participation in, and equal opportunities for, leadership at all levels of decision making in public, economic and political life.

5. Furthermore, violence against women is still prevalent. Statistics from 2008 to 2018 show that one in three women, or 736 million women globally, have been subject to physical and/or sexual violence at least once in their lifetime since age 15. Even in developed countries like the UK, sexual harrassment statistics run high. In 2021, an investigation by UN Women UK found that 97% of women aged 18 to 24 had previously been sexually harassed, with a further 96% of women not reporting such incidents due to the belief that any such report would be of no use. Tied in with poverty, an estimated 10 million girls would also be at risk of child marriages.

6. Thus, Target 5.2 hopes to eliminate all forms of violence - be it verbal, physical, or other, against women and girls in the public and private sphere. This includes sexual exploitation, trafficking and other situations in which females can be taken advantage of.

7. Target 5.3 was established to encourage and work towards the removal of all harmful practices like child, early or forced marriages and female genital mutilation. Other targets under Goal 5 also recognise the importance of social protection policies and other institutional measures that could be taken to help females.

Note: You do not need to know and remember every statistic. Just the major ones for each goal will do.

16. Using real world examples, discuss the effectiveness of foreign direct investment in achieving economic growth and economic development. (15)

<u>Introduction</u>

1. Foreign Direct Investments (FDIs) refer to long term investments in physical capital like machinery and factories, carried by foreign multinational corporations (MNCs) in a country.

2. Economic growth can refer to actual and/or potential economic growth. Actual economic growth occurs when there is an increase in the Aggregate Demand (AD) or Real Gross Domestic Product (RGDP) of the economy, usually over a year.

3. Potential economic growth occurs when there is an increase in the economy's capacity to produce at full employment, when operating at the given level of technology with all factors of production fully and efficiently utilised. The level of potential output has increased.

4. "Economic development" refers to a sustained improvement in the standard of living (SOL) of residents in a country. Both the material and non-material SOL are taken into account.

5. The material SOL of residents refers to the quantity of goods and services available to the population for consumption. It is typically measured via real national income per capita.

6. On the other hand, factors affecting the non-material SOL are more intangible aspects that contribute to quality of life. They are usually measured by health, environment, education and other indicators.

<u>Thesis 1: FDIs are effective in achieving actual economic growth and enabling the material SOL to increase, in turn improving economic development.</u>

1. $Aggregate\ Demand\ (AD) = (C) + (G) + (I) + (X - M)$, where (I) refers to Investments. With an increase in the level of FDI, the (I) component of AD would increase, shifting AD rightward.

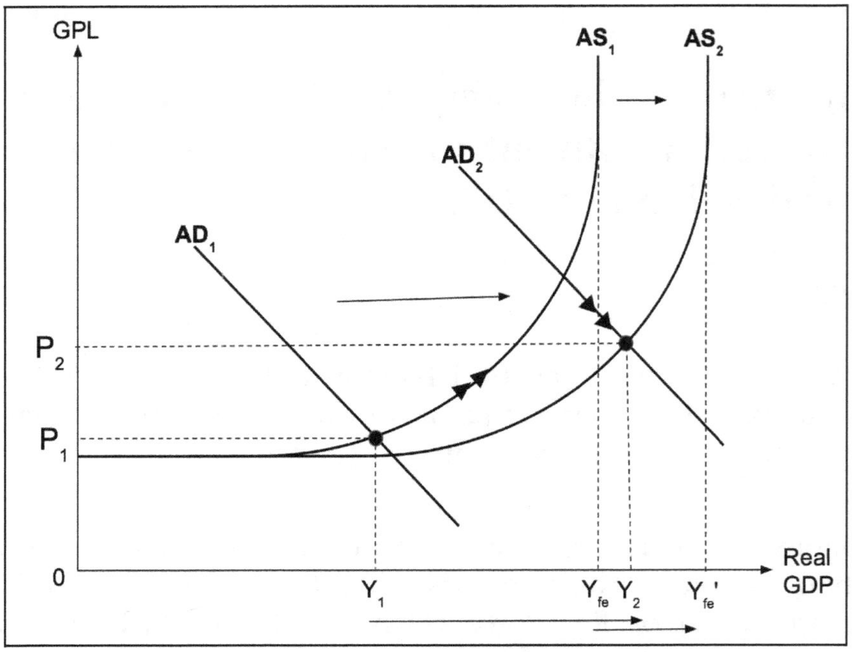

Fig 1: Effect of Increased (I) on RGDP and Real National Income

2. With more FDIs, more factor inputs such as labour and capital are being utilised. This enables owners of factors of production to earn higher incomes. For example, more workers (a derived-demand) would be hired, enabling workers to earn higher incomes. Others that own capital like machinery would be able to sell their equipment to the factories. Those who own plots of land would be able to collect rental incomes.

3. With factor owners earning greater incomes, their level of domestic consumption (C) would increase as well. Multiple rounds of spending and income generation would result in the AD shifting rightward more than proportionately to the initial injection into the circular flow of income caused by an influx of FDIs, from AD_1 to AD_2. This is known as the multiplier process.

4. This enables RGDP to increase more than proportionately to the initial increase in investment spending, enabling actual economic growth to be achieved.

5. For instance, from 2000 to 2008, the European Union (EU) was coined the "main beneficiary of FDI flows in world markets". In fact, Slovakia's (a member country of the EU) large FDI inflows from 2000 to 2008, especially in the "automotive, machinery and metal products, and electronics industries", was one of the reasons for its substantial increase in yearly economic growth from 1.2% in 2000 to 10.8% in 2007. Economic growth fell in 2008 to 5.6% due to the 2008 Financial Crisis.

<u>Thesis 2: FDIs are effective in achieving potential economic growth and enabling the non-material SOL to increase, in turn achieving economic development.</u>

1. Besides the improvement in actual economic growth, potential growth is achieved as well. An increase in the level of (I) would increase the capital stock in the economy. Furthermore, MNCs usually increase the state of technology in the economy, and enable knowledge and technological transfers to occur.

2. Referring to Fig 1, the above occurrences will shift the Long Run Aggregate Supply (LRAS) curve rightward from AS_1 to AS_2. This causes the full employment output to increase from Y_{fe} to Y_{fe}'.

3. With the productive capacity of the economy expanded, the economy would be able to produce a greater output at full employment. The level of potential output has thus increased.

4. As seen in Fig 1, combined increases in both the AD and AS cause the real national income in the economy to increase from Y_1 to Y_2. Hence, the presence of FDI helps to stimulate the economy by allowing both forms of economic growth to occur, enabling sustained economic growth to be achieved in the long run. Ceteris paribus, there would be an increase in real national income per capita, enabling the material standard of living and by extension, economic development, to be achieved.

5. For example, since 2003, yearly flows in FDIs from China to Africa have increased significantly from US $75 million in 2003, to a staggering US $5.4 billion in 2018, and a further US $4.2 billion in 2020. This has stimulated the previously-crippled African economy, where previously they lacked funding and technical know-how.

6. While Africa has a long way to go, researchers have confirmed that the investments and increase in capital stock which FDIs bring to an economy, can indeed be a means of "employment generation" and "poverty eradication".

7. Assuming that the FDI also occurs in infrastructure sectors like the telecommunications sector, it will boost efficiency and productivity. For example, with faster cellular communication, the digital connectivity between residents and with the rest of the world would increase. Besides enabling the productivity of workers, the greater ease of communication would increase convenience and enhance the quality of life of residents, thus improving economic development as well.

Antithesis 1: FDIs are ineffective in directly achieving economic growth and economic development, as most benefits are reaped by the foreign MNCs instead of the domestic economy.

1. In the case of China's FDI in Africa, many job opportunities are given to Chinese workers instead of Africans. These Chinese workers repatriate much of their income back to their homeland instead of spending within Africa. Therefore, the economic boost to Africa is much smaller than expected.

2. Furthermore, with the introduction of new technology to aid production, and subsequent technological diffusion, workers in the domestic countries may be left structurally unemployed as their jobs become increasingly automated.

3. This is because the unemployed may lack the essential skills needed to find jobs in other industries, as there is a skills mismatch where labour skills in demand by employers are not the skills which these retrenched workers possess.

Antithesis 2: FDIs may directly harm economic growth and development, as foreign MNCs may exploit resources found in the country.

1. When unscrupulous MNCs conduct FDI in other countries, there is a risk that the MNCs will run the country dry - exploiting its resources as quickly as possible and without regard for the environment. In the long term, this would decrease the quantity and quality of the factors of production available.

2. Instead of benefitting the lives of residents in Africa, China has been accused of 'exploiting' Africa and its vast quantities of natural resources, under the pretext of conducting FDIs.

3. With 30% of the world's hydrocarbon and mineral reserves, and other raw materials like sugar, salt, gold, uranium, diamonds, timber, cocoa beans and petroleum, African nations are attractive to the Chinese, who require natural resources to expand their manufacturing capacity.

4. With fewer natural resources of a substandard quality as a result of over-exploitation, economic growth will be less sustainable as the productive capacity of the economy shrinks. Sustainability refers to the ability of the country to meet the needs of the present generation without compromising on the ability to meet the needs of future generations.

5. Africa is host to incredible biodiversity in the rich tropical rainforests, deserts, savannahs, grasslands and wetlands. The millions of species of flora and fauna provided sources of food, medicine, water, and other valuable resources for the African people to thrive.

6. However, due to the over-exploitation of its natural resources, Africa is estimated to lose about half its mammals and birds, with regions like the

Democratic Republic of Congo and Cote d'Ivoire being severely affected. This, coupled with environmental issues like water and air pollution from MNCs' factories spewing toxic waste, heavy metals and plastics, environmental degradation in Africa is particularly dire.

7. Besides hindering sustainable economic growth, this would also make Africa more unlivable for its residents, and cause widespread health problems like lung cancer to arise, as the air pollution becomes worse. Overall, both the material and non-material SOL for residents would deteriorate.

8. Hence, such FDIs would eventually decrease both the material and non-material standards of living of residents in the country, harming economic development.

Concluding Section

1. In conclusion, when implemented properly, FDIs can be a big help in stimulating economic growth and development through increasing the level of (I), capital stock and technical know-how in the economy. There are numerous other benefits to FDIs as well, such as the creation of jobs domestically and an increase in the productivity of workers in the economy due to knowledge acquisition and technological transfer.

2. However, the extent of economic growth and development following the FDIs would be highly dependent on the exact terms and conditions of the FDIs, and the policies put in place by the local government to regulate such FDIs.

3. For instance, governments can mandate that a certain percentage of job openings created by the presence of such FDIs, be given to domestic workers. This would ensure that the domestic economy reaps the benefits of economic growth.

4. The government could also impose rules and regulations to ensure that FDIs are mindful of worker and environmental protection, enabling sustained economic growth and economic development to be achieved in the domestic economy.

5. The government should therefore keep tabs on firms conducting the FDIs, and implement regular checks to ensure that profit-motivated firms do not simply exploit natural resources or workers in the domestic country. Should any firms be found flouting the regulations, penalties can be meted out.

6. With measures put in place to regulate the MNCs conducting FDI in the domestic country, there would be a greater assurance that such FDIs would stimulate economic growth and economic development in the domestic economy, and that the potentially harmful effects of unregulated FDI do not come to pass or are at the very least, mitigated.

17. Using real world examples, evaluate the success of a country of your choice in achieving any two Sustainable Development Goals. (15)

Introduction

1. The 17 Sustainable Development Goals (SDGs) are a set of indicators and their respective targets which the United Nations (UN) has pledged to achieve, in accordance with the "2030 Agenda for Sustainable Development".

2. These 17 SDGs were adopted by all UN member states in 2015, and serve as an immediate call to action for both developed and developing countries to embark on a worldwide partnership to tackle individual socioeconomic problems faced by many countries. This includes but is not limited to: poverty, health, education, inequality, other deprivations, a lack of economic growth, climate change and the preservation of wildlife.

3. It is hoped that achieving the 17 SDGs would increase a country's economic development. Economic development refers to a sustained improvement in the standard of living of residents, comprising the material standard of living - typically measured by the real national income per capita, as well as the non-material standard of living - better health and environmental standards, and education opportunities.

4. In this essay, the success of Costa Rica in achieving two of the SDGs will be analysed.

SDG 12 - Responsible Consumption and Production

1. As global consumption and production rates continually increase to drive economic growth in countries, natural resources continue to be depleted at an unsustainable rate. The natural environment also suffers from serious degradation. "Sustainability" refers to the ability to meet the needs of the present generation without compromising on the ability to meet the needs of future generations.

2. Hence, SDG 12 is about responsible consumption and production. Target 12.2 calls for the "sustainable management and efficient use of natural resources" by 2030. Target 12.4 called for the "environmentally sound management of chemicals and all wastes throughout their life cycle, in accordance with agreed international frameworks, and significantly reduce their release to air, water and soil in order to minimise their adverse impacts on human health and the environment" by 2020.

3. Target 12.5 asks that countries "substantially reduce waste generation through prevention, reduction, recycling and reuse" by 2030. Target 12.B asks for countries to "develop and implement tools to monitor sustainable development impacts for sustainable tourism that creates jobs and promotes local culture and products".

Thesis 1: Costa Rica has been successful in working towards achieving SDG 12 - Responsible Consumption and Production.

1. As of 2022, Costa Rica has been "on track" to achieve SDG 12, according to the Sustainable Development Report 2022.

2. In fact, as of 2022, Costa Rica has already achieved success in some indicators, such as: controlling its "production-based SO_2 emissions" (achieved by 2018), "SO_2 emissions embodied in imports" (achieved by 2018), "production-based nitrogen emissions" (achieved by 2015), "nitrogen emissions embodied in imports" (achieved by 2015), and "non-recycled municipal solid waste" (achieved by 2019).

3. Hence, Costa Rica has shown much progress and success in achieving many of the indicators in SDG 12. Success in fulfilling those indicators directly helps with achieving Targets 12.4 about controlling the release of hazardous chemicals, as well as Target 12.5 regarding reducing waste generation.

4. In relation to Targets 12.2 and 12.B, Costa Rica is an example to follow in its sustainable management of resources, while simultaneously capitalising on this to achieve economic growth. Costa Rica has been the pioneer and trailblazer of "ecotourism". It is able to earn a profit from tourists who come to explore its wildlife and biodiversity, but in return, it has to ensure that its national parks and areas remain protected, in line with its tourism industry's worldwide reputation for being "environmentally friendly".

5. This has led to nearly half a million acres of land in Costa Rica being designated as "protected areas". Conservation of natural resources is also prioritised. With a flourishing ecotourism industry came the shutting down of logging industries and the like; Costa Rican employees in these industries were re-employed in the ecotourism industry instead. This puts Costa Rica in a strong position for the fulfilment of Target 12.2 and 12.B.

Antithesis 1: Costa Rica has not been successful in working towards achieving SDG 12 - Responsible Consumption and Production.

1. Costa Rica still requires much improvement with respect to other indicators for SDG 12. It faces "major challenges" in controlling its level of "electronic waste", and "challenges remain" in limiting its "exports of plastic waste". This directly contests its ability to fulfil Target 12.5.

2. Some have also contested that the ecotourism industry has brought about more environmental and sustainability harm, than benefits. Given that firms in the tourism industry are still largely profit-motivated, protection of the Costa Rican environment and its natural resources could in some cases have taken a backseat in attempts to cut corners to maximise profits.

3. This is due to a phenomenon known as the Tragedy of the Commons, a situation involving Common Access Resources - natural resources or "gifts of nature" that do not have ownership rights and are hence non-excludable but rivalrous in nature - whereby individual consumers, acting independently according to their own self-interests, behave contrary to the common good of all users by depleting a resource through their collective action, affecting sustainability of the resources for future generations.

4. As such, some believe that Costa Rica is becoming a "prime example of ecotourism gone wrong", due to corruption and a shortage of finances, environmental enforcement and expertise. These factors make it extremely difficult for Costa Ricans to continue to protect their natural environment. This has led to many environmental issues like habitat disruption of flora and fauna, and numerous cases of pollution and litter. If such issues cannot be resolved, it would impinge on Costa Rica's ability to fulfil Targets 12.2 and 12.B, and by extension, SDG 12 as a whole.

<u>SDG 5 - Gender Equality and Empowering All Women and Girls</u>

1. SDG 5 promotes gender equality and the empowerment of women. Gender equality refers to the act of giving both males and females equal health, educational, economic, political and other opportunities.

2. Female empowerment refers to the elimination of discrimination faced by women and girls regarding access to education, healthcare, and in other spheres of social and economic life - for example, access to credit. It also includes the view of gender equality, where women and girls have access to equal opportunities as men and boys, achieving their potential to lead a fulfilling and productive life.

3. Target 5.1 highlights the importance of ending all types of discrimination against females in all places. Target 5.2 hopes to eliminate all forms of violence, be it verbal, physical or other, against women and girls in the public and private sphere. This includes sexual exploitation, trafficking and other situations in which females are taken advantage of.

4. Target 5.5 pledges to ensure women's full and effective participation in, and equal opportunities for, leadership at all levels of decision making in public, economic and political life.

5. Other targets under SDG 5 also recognise the importance of social protection policies and other institutional measures that could be taken to help females.

Thesis 2: Costa Rica has been successful in working towards achieving SDG 5 - Gender Equality and Empowering All Women and Girls.

1. As of 2022, Costa Rica has already able to achieve success in numerous indicators of SDG 5, such as that of "ratio of female-to-male mean years of education received" (achieved by 2019), the "seats held by women in national parliament" (achieved 2020), and the "gender wage gap" (achieved by 2018).

2. The fulfilment of these indicators contributes to Costa Rica's ability to fulfil Targets 5.1 and 5.5, and the fulfilment of SDG 5 as a whole.

3. Furthermore, according to the UN Women Data Hub, Costa Rica has actively put into practice 83.3% of their legal frameworks that aim to promote, enforce, and monitor gender equality under the SDG indicator. There is a focus on violence against women under these frameworks.

4. In 2011, the percentage of women aged 18 to 24 who were first married or in a union by the age of 18, was 21%. This has fallen to 17% in 2018. The number of adolescent births per 1,000 women aged 15 to 19 was 40.9 in 2019, which is a large decrease from 50.9 in 2018. This suggests a marked improvement for Costa Rican women following the establishment of the SDGs, in line with Targets 5.1 and 5.2.

5. In relation to Target 5.5, Costa Rica has also shown promise in terms of having an increased female representation in the political sphere. In February 2021, 46% of seats in parliament were held by women, up from 33% in 2015.

Antithesis 2: Costa Rica has not been successful in working towards achieving SDG 5 - Gender Equality and Empowering All Women and Girls.

1. In general, "challenges remain" with regards to Costa Rica's "moderately improving" progress for this Goal, according to the Sustainable Development Report 2022.

2. For instance, Costa Rica still faces difficulty in achieving the target "ratio of female-to-male labour force participation rate", casting doubt on its ability to fulfil Target 5.5 on increasing women's full participation in different spheres of life, respectively.

3. Furthermore, in 2018, 7.2% of women aged 15 to 49 have reported being subjected to physical and/or sexual violence by a current or former intimate partner in the last 12 months. There has reportedly been a difficulty in Costa Rica's ability to tackle the issue of physical and sexual harassment against women.

4. In addition, in 2018, women and girls aged 10 and above were reported to have spent 23.5% of their time on unpaid or domestic work, which is much

greater compared to 8.2% spent by men. Moreover, though 46% of parliamentary seats were held by women in 2021, which is higher than that in 2015 and many years prior, there has been little to no improvement from 2018 to 2021, where the percentage of seats held by women stagnated at 46%. This casts a doubt as to whether the proportion of women in parliament will continue to increase in the future.

Concluding Section

1. Statistically, Costa Rica has already fulfilled or is on track to fulfil many of the indicators in these two SDGs. However, it has to continue maintaining its progress amidst corrupt or profit-motivated entities who may detract from the common efforts of others to achieve the SDGs.

2. The Costa Rican government could consider implementing stronger enforcement measures and ensure that there are severe penalties to penalise those who flout national guidelines.

18. Distinguish between GDP and GNI per capita figures. (10)

Introduction

1. The standard of living of a population refers to the economic and social wellbeing of the residents of a country, and encompasses both the material and non-material standard of living (SOL).

2. In determining the material SOL in a country, Gross Domestic Product (GDP) or Gross National Income (GNI) per capita figures are typically calculated. This enables a country's GDP or GNI per capita over time to be measured, and allows for cross-country comparison as well.

3. The GDP is one method of calculating the value of income in the economy. It refers to the value of all final goods and services produced within the geographical boundary of a country's economy in a given time period, regardless of the nationality of the owners of the factors of production.

4. On the other hand, the GNI is the total income received by the country from its residents and firms, regardless of whether these factors of production and assets are located within the geographical boundary of the country or abroad.

5. GDP and GNI per capita both reflect the national income of a country divided by its total population. This reflects the standard of living of an average resident more accurately than simply using GDP or GNI figures of the country, as it takes the population size into account.

6. If GDP or GNI increases, but the population size increases in tandem, the GDP or GNI per capita may remain constant, or even decrease.

Main Difference: Geographical Boundary versus Nationality

1. While GDP only accounts for the value of all final goods and services produced within the geographical boundary of a country, GNI values all goods and services produced by the factors of production which its residents own, regardless of where the factors inputs are being utilised for production.

2. For example, profits earned by Japanese-owned factories located in Singapore would be counted in the GDP of Singapore and the GNI of Japan, but their value would not be counted in either the GDP of Japan or GNI of Singapore.

Hence, $GNI = GDP + net\ incomes\ from\ abroad$

3. Such incomes repatriated from abroad could encompass that earned by multinational corporations (MNCs) engaging in inward Foreign Direct Investments (FDIs) by owning firms and factories in a foreign country and generating profits through entrepreneurship. Though profits generated by inward FDIs may be included in the GDP per capita figures of the country in which it is conducted, such incomes are typically repatriated back to the country from which the MNC originates.

4. Other incomes which may be repatriated to the home countries of owners of the factor inputs also include but are not limited to: rental incomes from owning property overseas, interest from hot money investments, dividends from stocks and share ownership overseas, and wages from workers who work abroad to send money back to their families at home.

5. As such, *net incomes from abroad* would simplistically encompass: net flow of profits + net flow of rental incomes + net flow of interest and dividends + net flow of wages, into the domestic country.

6. If there were to be a net inflow of income, the country's GNI per capita figure would be higher than the GDP per capita figure. Should there be a net outflow of income, the GNI per capita figure would be lower than the GDP per capita figure.

7. As such, distinct differences in certain countries' GNI per capita vs GDP per capita may arise. This is because certain nations, especially developing countries, often see a greater extent of inward FDIs into their country, rather than outward investments by their own local firms into foreign countries.

8. For instance, in 2018, Botswana's GNI per capita was US $7,340, which was lower than its GDP per capita of US $8,279. In the same year, Mozambique's GNI per capita was US $460, while its GDP per capita was US $503. Similar trends where GNI per capita figures are lower than GDP per capita figures, are seen in some other developing nations, including Chad, Kenya and Uganda.

9. On the other hand, countries with a higher or similar GNI per capita compared to GDP per capita include many developed nations. In 2018, the USA's GNI per capita was US $63,510, compared to its GDP per capita of US $63,064. Liechtenstein's GNI per capita was US $186,064, while its GDP per capita was US $180,366.

10. For countries with higher GNI per capita figures, it is likely that the level of inward investment is lower than that of outward investment, as more profits are repatriated back to the domestic country from abroad, than are repatriated to foreign countries by factors of production located in the domestic country.

11. Hence, at the end of the day, especially for developing nations, the GNI per capita figure is likely more accurate in depicting the level of real national

income per capita and hence, the material SOL, compared to the GDP per capita figure which may overestimate the material SOL of the country.

12. However, for developed countries in general, as seen in the figures above, GDP and GNI tend to be largely similar and thus either can be quite similarly used to measure the level of material SOL in the country.

19. Using real world examples, discuss the strengths and limitations of two different approaches to measuring economic development. (15)

Introduction

1. "Economic development" refers to a sustained improvement in the standard of living (SOL) of residents in a country. Both the material and non-material SOL of residents are taken into account.

2. The material SOL of residents refers to the quantity of goods and services available to the population for consumption. It is typically measured via real national income per capita.

3. On the other hand, factors affecting the non-material SOL are more intangible aspects that contribute to quality of life. They are usually measured by health, environment, education and other indicators.

4. Composite indicators, unlike single indicators, use more than one measure to ascertain the level of economic development of a country; a country's performance across an assortment of single indicators is calculated to give a single combined figure.

5. Two such composite indicators are the Human Development Index (HDI) and Inclusive Development Index (IDI).

Human Development Index (HDI)

1. The HDI is a composite indicator that measures economic development across three different dimensions: Purchasing-Power-Parity-adjusted Real Gross National Income per capita (material welfare), life expectancy at birth (non-material welfare: health standards), and mean and expected years of schooling (non-material welfare: education standards).

2. A single figure is derived and can then be used for comparison between countries, as well as for a particular country, across a certain time period.

3. In 2019, Norway ranked first globally with a HDI of 0.957, followed by Ireland and Switzerland which tied at 0.955. In contrast, the Central African Republic and Niger had the lowest HDI figures, 0.397 and 0.394 respectively.

Strength 1: The HDI is a simple yet rather comprehensive and accurate composite indicator that can be used to measure the relative material SOL of a single country over time, as well as across different countries for comparison.

1. The HDI uses Purchasing Power Parity-adjusted Real Gross National Income per capita (PPP-adjusted Real GNI per capita) as a proxy for a country's relative material SOL. The choice of this indicator is one of the HDI's strengths for various reasons.

Use of GNI over GDP Values

1. Gross National Income (GNI) is the total income received by the country from its residents and firms, regardless of whether these factors of production and assets are located within the geographical boundary of the country or abroad.

2. Compared to another measure used to measure national income, Gross Domestic Product (GDP), the GNI figures are arguably more accurate in measuring the material SOL.

2. This is because in certain countries, especially developing countries, there is a greater extent of inward investment by foreign multinational corporations (MNCs) into the country, rather than outward investments by its own local firms into foreign countries.

3. Hence, calculating GDP, which accounts for the value of all final goods and services produced within the geographical boundary of a country only, would tend to result in an overestimation of the national income levels of such countries, as incomes earned from these investments are typically repatriated back to the country from which the MNC originates.

4. Alternatively, developing countries may actually receive more inward income remittances from its workers working overseas. As this may significantly contribute to the material SOL of residents, GNI figures could actually be higher than GDP figures in some cases. Hence, using GDP figures would understate the material SOL of the country. One such example of this is The Philippines.

5. Hence, the GNI provides a more accurate measure of national income, which can then be used for cross-country comparison to determine the relative material SOL in countries.

Use of GNI per capita figures instead of merely calculating GNI

1. On top of using GNI figures over GDP figures, "per capita" figures are used. The GNI per capita refers to the national income of a country divided by the total population size of the country. This reflects the standard of living of an average resident more accurately than simply calculating the GNI of a country, as it takes into account changes in population size.

2. This is because if the GNI increases, but the population size increases in tandem, the GNI per capita may remain constant or even decrease; the average material SOL would not increase.

<u>Use of Real GNI per capita figures instead of merely GNI per capita</u>

1. "Real" GNI per capita suggests that figures have been adjusted for inflation by referencing it to chosen nominal base year prices, thus providing a more accurate picture as to the change in real purchasing power of residents over the years, in spite of inflation.

<u>Use of PPP-adjusted figures</u>

1. Lastly, using "PPP-adjusted" real GNI per capita figures allow for more accurate cross-country comparison, as they account for differences in the cost of living by equalising and standardising the purchasing power of currencies across all countries. This standardisation is achieved by comparing hundreds of prices of goods from a common "basket of goods" that is representative of what the average resident consumes.

2. Hence, with the nominal GNI per capita converted into PPP-adjusted real GNI per capita figures, different countries' relative material SOL can now be more accurately compared.

<u>Analysis of 2019 HDI Data</u>

1. Comparing the breakdown of the 2019 HDI data between the Netherlands and Australia who both tied 8th with a HDI of 0.944, the Netherlands' PPP-adjusted real GNI per capita at $57,707 (2017 $PPP), which is much higher than that of Australia's at $48,085 (2017 $PPP).

2. Hence, the average real income earned by a resident of the Netherlands, independent of where the income was generated, was much higher than that of a resident in Australia. This translates into the average Netherlander having higher purchasing power - being able to purchase a greater quantity of goods and services - compared to the average Australian. The average Netherlander likely has a greater material SOL than the average Australian.

<u>Strength 2: The HDI considers crucial social (health, education) factors when measuring economic development.</u>

1. The HDI identifies crucial factors which contribute to perceivable differences in the non-material standards of living between countries, and incorporates this into the matrix for determining the relative HDI values of countries. This gives a more comprehensive picture of economic development.

2. Continuing from the above comparison between Australia and the Netherlands, both countries have the same HDI at 0.944, despite the Netherlands outperforming Australia in terms of the material SOL. This is due to Australia surpassing the Netherlands in non-material SOL indicators like the "Life Expectancy at Birth", "Expected Years of Schooling", and "Mean Years of Schooling".

3. Regarding the "Life Expectancy at Birth", The Netherlands' is 82.3 while Australia's is 83.4, giving Australia a slight edge. Furthermore, though the "Mean Years of Schooling" are highly similar (Netherlands: 12.4, Australia: 12.7), the "Expected Years of Schooling" differ. Netherlands' figure stands at 18.5 years while Australia's stands at 22.0. This seems to suggest that the Australian residents are given more education opportunities than Netherlands residents. As education is seen as a critical enabler to a better life, this explains why overall, Australia is considered on par with the Netherlands despite the higher average income in the latter.

4. Hence, the HDI has significant strengths in being able to provide rather accurate and comprehensive cross-country and cross-time comparisons that encompass both the material and non-material SOL.

<u>Limitation 1: The HDI is unable to account for economic or social inequalities that exist between certain demographics in a country.</u>

1. <u>Economic Inequality:</u>

   In 2019, South Africa had a HDI of 0.709, with a recorded PPP-adjusted real GNI per capita of $12,129 (2017 PPP$). However, in reality, there is rampant income inequality in South Africa. The top 1% of earners account for 20% of the country's national income, and the top 10% take home 65%, leaving the remaining 90% of the population a mere 35% of real national income.

2. Hence, the HDI does not accurately depict the SOL of a typical South African resident, who may in reality have a real per capita income much lower than $12,129 (2017 PPP$).

3. <u>Social Inequality:</u>

   South Africa's "Expected Years of Schooling" and "Mean Years of Schooling" were 13.8 and 10.2 respectively in 2019. However, in actuality, the number of expected and mean years of schooling differ greatly depending on the demographic of the individual resident.

4. Remnants of the abolished South African apartheid system gives rise to racial discrimination possibly favouring Caucasian South Africans being recipients of quality education.

5. Girls are put at a significant disadvantage in receiving education compared to boys, given the heavily-patriarchal society which de-emphasises the role of education in a woman's life, and emphasises instead the female's role of caregiver in the household.

6. Moreover, certain healthcare issues are more prevalent amongst particular demographics. In 2019, South Africa had the highest number of people living with Acquired Immunodeficiency Syndrome (AIDS) or Human Immunodeficiency Virus (HIV), at 7.1 million.

7. Statistically, females in South Africa were four times as likely to develop HIV compared to males. This not only suggests a gender health disparity that the HDI does not account for, but it also implies a domino-effect that results in inequalities in other social indicators. Girls are often unable to complete their education as a result of contracting HIV, preventing them from earning higher incomes in the future.

8. In this instance, it could mean that the HDI's health, education and national income indicators heavily overestimate the actual material and non-material SOL for females in South Africa.

9. Hence, the HDI is unable to account for both economic and social inequalities, given that only average figures are presented in the data.

<u>Limitation 2: The HDI does not take many other social issues into account.</u>

1. One of the largest criticisms of the HDI is the fact that it does not incorporate other important social factors, including issues like the extent or presence (or lack thereof) of certain civil liberties associated with Western democracies.

2. These would include issues like the right to vote or universal suffrage, which may not be present in all countries. For example, a women's right to vote is not practised in Saudi Arabia and the Vatican City. Other issues of civil liberty include the right to the freedom of speech, which is greatly restricted in countries like China and North Korea through heavy monitoring and censorship on social media and other platforms, and the implementation of numerous firewalls.

3. Other factors which the HDI neglects include exposure to crime, violence, and environmental degradation. For example, despite Italy ranking very highly with a HDI of 0.892 in 2019, it is notorious for counts of petty crimes (pickpocketing, car burglary, scams, purse-snatching etc.) experienced by both locals and tourists, as well as other serious forms of organised crime, like that executed by the Sicilian Mafia, an infamous crime syndicate.

Inclusive Development Index (IDI)

1. The Inclusive Development Index is a composite indicator measuring 103 countries' yearly standings with respect to 11 different dimensions (also called "national key performance indicators" or "sub-pillars") of economic progress, on top of their respective GDP performances.

2. The IDI has three pillars: "Growth and Development", "Inclusion", and "Intergenerational Equity and Sustainability", the last of which refers to the sustainable stewardship of natural and financial resources.

3. Under "Growth and Development", the national key performance indicators (KPIs) include: Real GDP per capita, Employment, Labour Productivity, and Health Life Expectancy. Under "Inclusion", the national KPIs are: Median Household Income, Poverty Rate, Income Gini and Wealth Gini. Lastly, that of "Intergenerational Equity and Sustainability" encompasses: Adjusted Net Savings, Public Debt (as a share of GDP), Dependency Ratio, and Carbon Intensity of GDP.

4. A country's IDI score can range between 1 and 7, with 1 representing the 'least inclusive' and 7 representing the 'most inclusive' in terms of economic development.

5. As such, the IDI aims to determine the level of sustainable and inclusive economic progress achieved by a country.

6. In 2018, Norway was ranked 1st on the IDI with a score of 6.08, closely followed by Iceland and Luxembourg (6.07 respectively). Many other Scandinavian countries, and a handful of European nations, also rank highly. All of the G7 countries ranked 27th or above, with Italy ranking 27th.

Strength 1: The IDI emphasises the level of sustainable economic progress made by a country.

1. The main goal of the IDI is to determine the level of sustainable and inclusive economic progress achieved by a country. This is more beneficial in projecting the sustained, long term economic growth that can be expected from a country, compared to making projections merely based on the current real GDP or GNI per capita figures, for multiple reasons.

2. Under the "Intergenerational Equity and Sustainability" pillar which relates to the sustainable stewardship of natural and financial resources, national KPIs include: Adjusted Net Savings, Public Debt (as a share of GDP), Dependency Ratio, and Carbon Intensity of GDP.

3. Firstly, economic progress measured by the IDI is a better measure of the sustained long-term economic progress that can be expected of a country, as it would account for any short term booms in the economy or temporary bursts

of economic growth driven by unsustainable practices, like the overexploitation of natural resources. Sustainability refers to the ability to meet the needs of the present generation, without compromising on the ability to meet the needs of the future generations.

4. For example, Brazil's overexploited natural resources have led to environmental problems like widespread deforestation, illegal poaching of wildlife, water pollution caused by excessive mining activities, oil spills, etc. In 2018, Brazil reported "high levels of resource depletion".

5. The IDI would therefore paint a more accurate picture of the economic progress of such countries in the future as well, rather than just providing figures for the annual "unsustainable" economic progress, which may then fluctuate greatly year-on-year.

6. However, Brazil was one of the notable exceptions for performing better than most developing countries in the "Inclusion" pillar, despite such high levels of resource depletion, as it compensated in another area - by having high levels of human capital investment.

<u>Strength 2: The IDI emphasises the level of inclusive, shared socioeconomic progress made by a country.</u>

1. Under the pillar "Inclusion", the national KPIs used include: Median Household Income, Poverty Rate, Income Gini and Wealth Gini. The IDI thus takes income inequality into account, unlike many of the other widely-used indicators like the HDI.

2. In 2018, the following countries were favoured for ensuring that their economic growth was more inclusive, and that the benefits of growth were not solely reaped by high income earners: Iceland, Nicaragua, New Zealand, Rwanda, South Korea and Vietnam.

3. In contrast, certain countries had significantly lower IDI score rankings than they did GDP per capita rankings, suggesting that their "growth had not translated to social inclusion". These include the USA, Japan, Nigeria and South Africa.

4. Since 2010, the USA has had a period of extensive economic growth that is referred to as the "longest economic expansion in USA history". However, in 2018, the USA's Gini index was 0.485. This was the "most inequitable level of income distribution recorded in the USA", and was the most inequitable income distribution figure out of all the G7 countries.

5. With regards to the Wealth Gini, the USA, in 2019, the wealthiest 1% in the country accounted for 40% of the country's 2019 net worth - the highest proportion of wealth held by the top 1% in the USA since 1989. Females, people of colour, the disabled, and communities in certain geographical areas

were amongst the demographics of people who may not have proportionately reaped the benefits of such extensive economic growth.

6. Hence, despite the USA being the world's leading economy, income inequality is prevalent, and benefits derived from economic growth do not necessarily translate into a higher material standard of living for the average resident.

7. After analysing the correlation between countries' real GDP per capita figures and IDI performance, a very weak correlation was found between the two. High real GDP per capita figures did not mean that the country would rank highly on IDI indicators, with the exception of certain indicators like the "Health Life Expectancy", "Labour Productivity", and the "Poverty Rate" for numerous advanced economies.

8. In fact, of the "top 11 countries in the top two quintiles of economic growth performance among advanced economies", only Israel, Korea and Iceland performed well on three or more national KPIs, with the others ranking poorly for those in the "Inclusion" pillar, or mediocre at best.

9. Hence, instead of simply relying on raw figures to demonstrate economic growth or the lack thereof, the IDI paints a more accurate picture as to whether the benefits of economic growth are even felt by the average resident in the country, or if the benefits are only concentrated in certain industries (e.g. export industries) or amongst higher income earners.

10. Therefore, the IDI more accurately illustrates the extent of sustainable, inclusive socioeconomic growth in a country, and whether such growth translates to a heightened standard of living for the average resident.

11. Following Strengths 1 and 2, it can be seen that the IDI is more comprehensive compared to many other indicators, including the HDI, as it goes beyond traditional measures of economic growth and development, and counteracts the limitations which traditional measures have presented in providing a more accurate analysis of the economic development of a country.

12. It accounts for the need for "sustainable economic growth" to drive economic development instead of merely being content with "economic growth" (Strength 1), and the need for "inclusive, shared economic progress" rather than one-sided growth in certain economic sectors only (Strength 2), none of which the HDI accounts for. In fact, the lack of such factors being taken into account has been a large critique of the HDI.

<u>Limitation 1: Many noteworthy countries' economies are omitted from the IDI due to the absence of historical data needed for cross-country comparison.</u>

1. Countries like Singapore, Kenya, Morocco and Cambodia are omitted from the IDI due to a lack of past data needed to establish the scores for certain national KPIs, specifically those which make up the "Inclusion" pillar.

2. Compared to the HDI which covers the figures of 189 countries, the IDI only covers that of 103 countries. This poses a significant disadvantage for the IDI in terms of not being able to fully compare the level of economic development between as extensive a number of different countries.

Limitation 2: IDI scores may not be strictly comparable across all countries.

1. Countries are sorted into one of two categories based on their overall IDI score - "Advanced Economies" or "Emerging Economies". Due to the varying nature of different economies, where some are considered "advanced" and others, "emerging", the IDI uses different definitions of poverty depending on the nature of the specific country's economy.

2. Hence, the "Poverty Rate" statistics reflected under the "Inclusion" pillar of each country cannot strictly be used in an apples-to-apples cross-country comparison, as those who fall under the definition of poverty in each country may simply not have been subjected to the same metrics.

3. Furthermore, it is unclear whether all national KPIs are weighted equally to give rise to a single IDI score. As certain countries may obtain better scores in some national KPIs over others, unequally weighted KPIs could potentially impact an accurate cross-country comparison of economic development based solely on the overall IDI score.

Limitation 3: The IDI fails to account for the level of education received by residents in a country, arguably omitting an important factor which can play an important role in the long-term economic development of a country.

1. Education is a critical factor in determining the level of inclusive development in a country, as it is viewed as an equaliser which enables the lower income households to break out of the poverty trap, a cycle that the poor are unable to get out of as their income remains unchanged or even worsens overtime. It is characterised by low incomes which give rise to low levels of education and healthcare. This results in low levels of human capital, low productivity, and the cycle of having low incomes repeats itself.

2. With a higher level of education in any given country, lower income households would be able to obtain higher levels of human capital, achieve higher productivity and earn higher incomes. Ceteris paribus, real per capita incomes would rise, enabling the material SOL to increase, allowing economic development to be achieved.

3. Furthermore, with higher incomes, economic growth would be further stimulated due to an increase in the levels of domestic consumption (C), spending and income generation in the economy, enabling economic development to occur as well. As such, the level of education in a country, potentially measured by indicators such as the "Adult Literacy Rate" of the

population, number of "Mean Years of Schooling" and "Expected Years of Schooling", would be good proxies for the level of sustainable economic growth and development in the long-term.

4. Hence, the exclusion of such a critical factor in the IDI, especially compared to other indicators like the HDI which include it, may detract from the IDI's credibility in being a comprehensive indicator that measures economic development.

Concluding Section

1. In conclusion, both these composite indicators are relatively more comprehensive in measuring the level of economic development in a country, compared to merely using single indicators.

2. As both the HDI and IDI have their limitations, they can be used hand-in-hand to counteract their individual limitations and provide an even more comprehensive understanding derived from cross-checking the data in both.

3. However, one thing is clear from the usage of both the HDI and IDI; an increase in real GDP or GNI per capita, though advantageous, may not necessarily translate to an increase in standard of living for the average resident, due to many other non-material factors that need to be taken into consideration, as well as whether the economic growth itself is sustainable and inclusive.

20. Using real world examples, discuss the significance of any two of the following as barriers to development: the informal economy, indebtedness, a weak institutional framework, lack of good governance and corruption. (15)

Introduction

1. "Economic development" refers to a sustained improvement in the standard of living (SOL) of residents in a country. Both the material and non-material SOL of residents are taken into account.

2. The material SOL of residents refers to the quantity of goods and services available to the population for consumption. It is typically measured via real national income per capita.

3. On the other hand, factors affecting the non-material SOL are more intangible aspects that contribute to quality of life. They are usually measured by health, environment, education and other indicators.

4. In this essay, the significance of "indebtedness" and the "lack of good governance and corruption" as barriers to development will be discussed.

5. Debt generally refers to money owed by individuals or organisations who have taken loans or borrowed in the past to finance expenditures. In this case, "indebtedness" is taken to refer to public debt, which refers to money owed by the government to local or foreign creditors.

6. A "lack of good governance" could refer to a government being negligent in its duties to improve the economic development of its country. "Good governance" can be defined as the leadership of a country possessing eight key characteristics: being "participatory, accountable, transparent, consensus-oriented, responsive, equitable and inclusive, effective and efficient, and lawful".

7. "Corruption" refers to the act of dishonestly abusing or exploiting one's position of power for personal gain instead of looking out for the welfare and best interest of the country's residents. "Corruption" often involves dishonest and fraudulent behaviour on the part of the government, and can come in a variety of forms, including but not limited to: accepting bribes, extortion, embezzlement of state funds, nepotism, and cronyism.

Indebtedness Thesis 1: Indebtedness serves as a barrier to economic development as it hinders improvement in the non-material SOL of residents.

1. Indebtedness often results in a lack of funds in the country, undermining the government's ability to finance the direct provision of merit goods and public goods, hindering the improvement of the SOL of residents, and by extension, economic development.

2. The "Third World Debt Crisis" occurred after the worldwide recession in the 1980s, where many developing nations who had previously borrowed money as a means of financing stopgap measures, or in the hopes of stimulating the economy in the short-term, were unable to repay their loans.

3. Any subsequent tax or government revenue earned would thus go towards debt servicing. Governments would be less able to finance essential services, merit goods like the direct provision of education and healthcare, and the provision of public goods like street lighting and other forms of infrastructure.

4. With fewer and lower quality healthcare services, the population may become more sickly due to insufficient or inadequate healthcare treatment. Mortality rates for infants (and adults) could skyrocket due to poor foetal-maternal and other healthcare, and the life expectancy of individuals at the time of birth would decrease. These factors would cause a decrease in the residents' non-material SOL.

5. For example, in 2021, Zimbabwe owed $10.5 billion debt to international financial institutions like the World Bank and African Development Bank. I 2020, the debt was already 86% of its Gross Domestic Product (GD Zimbabwe's mountain of unsustainable debt is one of the multiple reas why the country is unable to better its healthcare system. As a resul healthcare system is inadequate in catering to the needs of the resic overburdened by high numbers of malaria, tuberculosis, paediatri Human Immunodeficiency Virus (HIV) cases. As such, in 2020, Zimb adult mortality rate (ages 15 to 60) was 45.68 deaths per 100 people.

6. In some countries with an under-resourced education system as indebtedness, the number of Mean and/or Expected Years of Sch be adversely affected. The literacy rates of such populations wou large proportion of the population may be illiterate, unable to rea

7. Overall, the decrease in provision of essential services, healthcare would perpetuate the poverty trap, a cycle that the to get out of as their incomes remain unchanged or even With regards to economic development, the poverty trap is low incomes, which give rise to low levels of education a results in low levels of human capital, low productivity, an

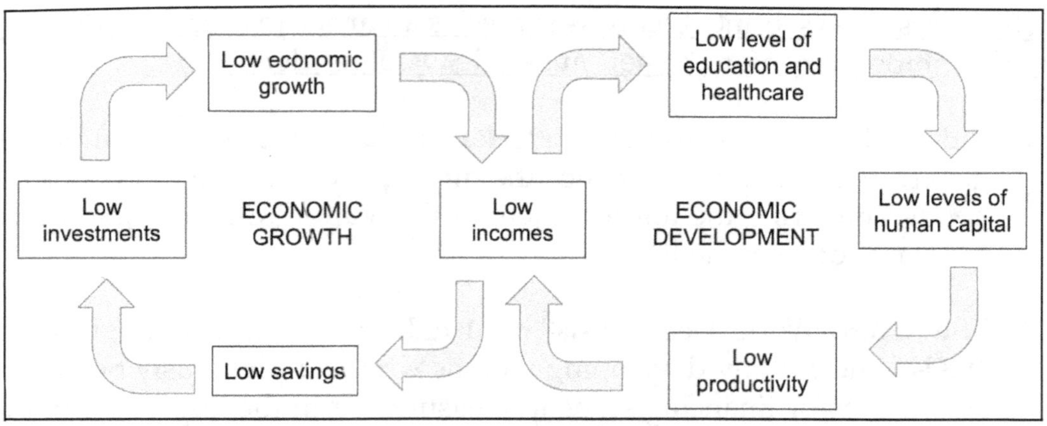

Fig 1: Poverty Trap

8. In addition, large levels of government debt would undermine the residents' trust in the government and its ability to plan its long-term finances. This may pose national security concerns if residents vocally and physically express their discontentment towards their government's perceived poor budget planning. For instance, in 2022 in Sri Lanka, residents took to the streets to riot and express their frustration about the country's US $25 billion skyrocketing debt which had plunged them into a severe economic crisis. Such socio-political instability further worsens economic development since it will deter investments and also create an unsafe place to live in.

<u>Indebtedness Thesis 2: Indebtedness serves as a barrier to economic development as it decreases the material SOL of residents in the country.</u>

1. Poor healthcare and education systems would result in a more sickly and unproductive workforce, reducing the full employment output and hindering economic growth from being achieved.

2. With reference to the poverty trap in Fig 1, low economic growth would result in low incomes, giving rise to low savings, low investments, and perpetuating the cycle of low economic growth. With lower levels of economic growth, households would face even lower levels of income. Ceteris paribus, real per capita incomes would fall, preventing the material SOL from improving.

3. Furthermore, foreign indebtedness may undermine the government's ability to finance the purchase of imports, which could include basic necessities such as food. This would have severe consequences on the material SOL of its citizens. In 2022, Sri Lanka's excessive debt levels resulted in difficulties in financially importing goods for its 22 million people; even daily essentials like fuel and food were in extremely short supply.

4. This could also extend to the inability to import certain factors of production (FOPs), increasing the unit cost of production of intermediate and final goods in an economy, decreasing the Short Run Aggregate Supply (SRAS) and leading to higher levels of inflation. Such inflation would erode the purchasing

power of residents. Moreover, the lack of factor inputs also means production and hence economic growth and economic development are hampered. For example, Sri Lanka's government declared in June 2022 that their "economy [had] collapsed" as there was almost no fuel and electricity, with the government "not even having $5 million to import gasoline", causing many "fuel ships [to be] anchored offshore, just waiting for cargos to be paid for".

Indebtedness Antithesis 1: Short-term indebtedness may be a necessary trade-off to achieve long-term economic development.

1. In the early stages of a country's industrialisation process and developmental transition from a primary-product-oriented to a manufacturing, capital-oriented economy, countries may require immediate funds to finance investments (I) and purchase of capital goods like machinery and production plants. This would help the country achieve long-term economic growth and development, given the increase in Aggregate Demand (AD) due to the rise in (I), and the increase in the Long Run Aggregate Supply (LRAS) due to the accumulation of capital stock in the economy.

2. This would normally necessitate loans being taken out by the government, incurring a short-term debt. However, after economic development has been achieved to a certain extent, the debt can be repaid, as rapid economic growth helps to increase the real national income of the country. Ceteris paribus, this would enable real per capita incomes to rise, increasing the material SOL for residents.

3. In the 1990s, the increased incidence of countries taking short-term debt with shorter maturities, was followed by higher incomes and greater levels of GDP growth. For example, research into the economic performance of the Association of Southeast Asian Nations (ASEAN) economies between the years 1995 to 2015 suggested that public debt did not adversely affect the economies of countries such as Indonesia, Thailand, Malaysia, the Philippines, and Vietnam. Rather, such debt was effectively used to finance public investments and thus actually promoted long-term economic growth and development.

4. Without the initial indebtedness which enables countries to purchase capital goods and finance investments, it may be extremely difficult to achieve long-term economic development, and the country's SOL may remain low.

Lack of Good Governance and Corruption Thesis 1: A lack of good governance and corruption would decrease the material SOL for residents.

1. The lack of any of the eight key aspects associated with good governance could threaten the economic growth and development of a country. For instance, a lack of accountability and transparency to the public regarding the use of government funds could result in members of the government illegally siphoning funds for their own use.

2. This is because the funds are leaked out of the economy instead of being used for legitimate purposes like the direct provision of merit or public goods, subsidisation of necessities for the poor and redistribution of income in the economy, or funding Research and Development (R&D) investment projects of state-owned enterprises to stimulate actual and potential economic growth.

3. Countries who have been ranked "most corrupt" on the Corruption Perception Index 2020/2021 - an index ranking countries based on their perceived level of corruption in the public sector - include Yemen, Venezuela, Somalia, Syria and South Sudan.

4. In South Sudan, corruption comprising frauds and other wrongdoings is widespread amongst high-ranking government officials, especially "government procurement officials within the ministry of finance and economic planning". Since 2005, government officials have been siphoning public funds in "broad daylight". From 2005 to 2012, an estimated $4 billion in state funds had reportedly been embezzled by officials. Such crimes typically go unpunished, with perpetrators almost never prosecuted. This is because even the investigations by the South Sudanese government into such alleged corruption are at times purposefully sabotaged.

5. The residents of the country would thus lose out due to decreases in the AD as a result of less money spent via government spending (G) to stimulate the economy.

6. Furthermore, with corruption comes an increased risk of government contracts not being honoured or firms incurring high costs due to the bribes required. This deters inward investments by multinational corporations (MNCs), reducing the level of (I) in the economy and affecting actual and potential growth. There is often also a diversion of funds away from crucial infrastructural investments, resulting in a lack of productivity growth.

7. All these results in a lack of economic growth, hindering the material SOL due to lower per capita incomes earned, ceteris paribus. This hinders economic development.

<u>Lack of Good Governance and Corruption Thesis 2: A lack of good governance and corruption would decrease the non-material SOL for residents.</u>

1. Corruption can also come in the form of turning a blind eye to firms who disobey governmental regulations, such as national environmental laws. Unscrupulous, profit-motivated firms would have the monetary incentive to exploit natural resources irresponsibly, due to a phenomenon known as the Tragedy of the Commons.

2. This is a situation involving Common Access Resources - natural resources or "gifts of nature" that do not have ownership rights and are hence

non-excludable but rivalrous in nature - whereby individual consumers, acting independently according to their own self-interests, behave contrary to the common good of all users by depleting a resource through their collective action, affecting the sustainability of the resources. Sustainability refers to the ability of the country to meet the needs of the present generation without compromising on the ability to meet the needs of future generations. Corrupt authorities may accept bribes in place of fining firms, and/or choose to ignore such violations.

3. Research has shown that a large part of deforestation globally has been occurring in developing countries in Latin America, Asia and Africa, and that there is an especially pronounced "strong positive relationship" between the extent of corruption in such countries, and the level of deforestation occuring. Further links have been established between the level of corruption and carbon dioxide emissions.

4. In 2001, the UN Food and Agricultural Organisation reported that corruption was one of the "main drivers" of deforestation in developing countries. In Indonesia for example, profit-motivated firms burn large areas of rainforests to obtain land for agriculture. Political elites have been infamous for protecting the firms from legal action in return for monetary benefits.

5. In other cases, the lack of good governance results in the release of large amounts of unregulated factory waste, like that of toxic fumes into the atmosphere, or chemicals into water bodies, causing air and land pollution. Much of the wildlife in the natural landscape may face a loss of habitat and be misplaced.

6. Furthermore, the release of toxic fumes would cause the natural environment to be less appealing. Breathing difficulties and other health issues like respiratory diseases, asthma and an increased incidence of lung cancer, may occur in badly-affected areas.

7. This decreases the non-material SOL for residents, hindering economic development. It also leads to long-term degradation of natural capital, hindering potential growth and long-term, sustainable economic development.

8. In contrast, countries with good governance and drastically fewer instances of corruption, notably Norway and Finland, have been deemed the "most environmentally-sustainable economies" by the Environmental Sustainability Index. Research suggested that "one of the strongest determinants [of an environmentally-sustainable economy], besides wealth... [is] good governance, including a broad commitment to the rule of law". In these countries, the non-material SOL of residents would be higher, enabling a greater level of economic development to be achieved.

Lack of Good Governance and Corruption Thesis 3: Oppressive regimes which limit civil liberties and individual freedoms may result in a decreased non-material SOL for residents.

1. In contrast with Western democracies where citizens are able to vote for their government during each election, and the tenure of the leader is capped to a maximum number of terms and/or years, in authoritarian regimes, those in power tend to stay in power for an extended period of time.

2. In countries run by a Dictatorship, like in the case of Russia and North Korea, residents may be given few civil liberties, live in a state of constant surveillance, and experience restrictions on individual freedoms.

3. Arguably, this may affect a resident's ability to uphold a fulfilling non-material SOL, as some may be unable to realise their full potential and individual liberties as human beings. For example, North Korea is almost completely cut out from the outside world. With a monopoly over North Korean media and the absence of the international press, the government can spread propaganda via the cartoons and documentaries it broadcasts, indoctrinating citizens with pro-government ideologies and anti-Western sentiments.

4. During elections, there is often only one option on the ballot. As the totalitarian regime prevents citizens from self-actualising or pursuing individualism through making their own personal decisions on aspects of life which have been shown to better the quality of an individual's life, one could argue that the non-material SOL of residents has decreased as a result.

5. Furthermore, corruption may occur in authoritative regimes as well, due to the absolute power which the leader wields, causing the same problems as described in the "Lack of Good Governance and Corruption Thesis 1 and 2".

Lack of Good Governance and Corruption Antithesis 1: The material SOL and by extension, economic development, may be helped, and not hindered, by authoritarian regimes that stay in power.

1. Though the oppression of individual liberties is significant in diminishing the non-material SOL of the country, one could argue that there is a greater incentive for leaders to ensure sustained economic growth in authoritarian regimes, rather than democracies. This could mean a better material SOL in authoritarian regimes compared to democracies.

2. Comparing a democracy where the ruling political party changes every few years, versus an autocracy where the leader or dictator stays in power for many years, research has found that corruption in some countries, specifically autocracies, may actually provide "greater economic freedom" that is "good for investments and growth".

3. This is supposedly evidenced by the "East Asian Paradox", where many East and Southeast Asian countries prospered economically, despite being run by dictators, authoritative regimes or corrupt, bribe-taking governments.

4. This is mainly because the staying power of the authoritative regimes empower firms with the confidence to invest, knowing that the ruling party that may have accepted bribes from them, will likely see the promised deals through in his term, or face backlash in the long-term for not doing so. In exchange for kickbacks, these firms may also receive advantages such as monopoly rights, which incentivises their investments.

5. This contrasts with democracies, where the credibility of politicians who commit to deals with firms is weakened, as the consequences of them not delivering are less harmful due to their short tenure. With this, firms in autocracies will be more willing to take on greater investments. Both actual and potential economic growth will be achieved, increasing the material SOL of residents, and the level of economic development in the country.

Concluding Section

1. In general, countries who are both in debt and have poor governance and rampant corruption are unlikely to undergo tremendous economic development than those without, ceteris paribus.

2. However, in determining which barrier to economic development is more significant, one could compare the list of most indebted countries and most corrupt countries, and determine how they fare in terms of economic development.

3. For example, two of the most corrupt countries in the world, Syria and South Sudan, were ranked 151st and 185th respectively out of 189 countries in the 2019 Human Development Index (HDI).

4. Countries among those most indebted (highest debt-to-GDP ratio) include Japan and Greece, who ranked 19th and 32nd respectively.

5. Hence, one could argue that indebtedness is not as significant a measure in hindering economic development, compared to a lack of good governance and corruption. However, this still largely depends on what the borrowed funds are used for and the effectiveness of the development strategies implemented. These, in fact, would largely depend on the quality of governance, suggesting that the two factors are highly intertwined.

www.ingramcontent.com/pod-product-compliance
Lightning Source LLC
LaVergne TN
LVHW082355200926
848481LV00012B/3573
* 9 7 8 9 8 1 1 8 5 4 9 5 8 *